Postmodern Consumer Research
The Study of Consumption as Text

For Ray and Sally,
With Love

Postmodern Consumer Research
The Study of Consumption as Text

Elizabeth C. Hirschman
Morris B. Holbrook

**Published in Cooperation With the
Association for Consumer Research**

SAGE Publications
International Educational and Professional Publisher
Newbury Park   London   New Delhi

For information address:

SAGE Publications, Inc.
2455 Teller Road
Newbury Park, California 91320

SAGE Publications Ltd.
6 Bonhill Street
London EC2A 4PU
United Kingdom

SAGE Publications India Pvt. Ltd.
M-32 Market
Greater Kailash I
New Delhi 110 048 India

Printed in the United States of America

Library of Congress Cataloging-in-Publication Data

Hirschman, Elizabeth.
    Postmodern consumer research: the study of consumption as text /
Elizabeth C. Hirschman, Morris B. Holbrook.
        p.   cm.
    Includes bibliographical references and index.
    ISBN 0-8039-4742-9.—ISBN 0-8039-4743-7 (pbk.)
        1. Consumers—Research. 2. Knowledge, Theory of—History.
I. Holbrook, Morris B.   II. Title.
    HF5415.3.H57   1992
    658.8'34—dc20   92-16460
                                                                  CIP

92 93 94 95 10 9 8 7 6 5 4 3 2 1

Sage Production Editor: Megan M. McCue

CONTENTS

PREFACE

This book traces a continuum of epistemological positions and validity issues back to philosophical questions that stem from the Cartesian dualism between mind and matter. Each philosophical stance along this continuum corresponds to a methodological orientation applicable to consumer research. In this, the criteria for assessing the value of an inquiry parallel the underlying epistemologies. We advocate the need for greater tolerance toward the divergent perspectives of consumer researchers approaching their work from a variety of directions.

In preparing this book, we have received help from many people. In particular, we thank Sally Holbrook, John O'Shaughnessy, Julie Ozannne, and Barbara Stern for their valuable comments on an earlier draft of this book. We also express our gratitude to the publications committee of the Association for Consumer Research. Morris Holbrook gratefully acknowledges the support of the Columbia Business School's Faculty Research Fund.

1

INTRODUCTION

Social revolution rolled across the continent. . . . The ideologies on which order had customarily depended, the cultural values by which it ruled, were also in deep turmoil. Science seemed to have dwindled to a sterile positivism, a myopic obsession with the categorizing of facts; philosophy appeared torn between such a positivism on one hand, and an indefensible subjectivism on the other; forms of relativism . . . were rampant.

(Eagleton, 1983, p. 54)

This passage taken from Eagleton describes European intellectual life in the wake of the First World War but in many respects offers an apt description of the conceptual and methodological choices now confronting consumer research. Over the past decade, a series of articles has seriously questioned the continued reliance of consumer research on positivistic, neopositivistic, or quasi-positivistic modes of inquiry (e.g., Anderson, 1983, 1986, 1989; Deshpande, 1983; Hirschman, 1986; Holbrook & O'Shaughnessy 1988; Holbrook, Bell, & Grayson, 1989; Mick, 1986; Ozanne & Hudson, 1989; Peter & Olson, 1983, 1989). Although these challenges do not speak with a unified

1

voice, they share deep concerns over issues related to the nature of knowledge in the study of consumption phenomena.

An implicit theme running through these postpositivistic or postmodern approaches to research deals with problems of epistemology that arise from questioning the connection of knowledge to empiricist moorings in a real world. If knowledge does not originate in some reality "out there," where does it come from? What rules guide its development, comprehension, description, and organization? Many of those who most oppose the abandonment of neopositivism, logical empiricism, or the received view center their arguments in the natural fear of scientific anarchy (Calder & Tybout, 1987, 1989; Hunt, 1989; Muncy & Fisk, 1987). They argue that relinquishing the metaphysical belief in one world with one truth about one reality precipitates an inevitable free-for-all or a free-fall into radical relativism wherein no hope of scientific consensus exists and no rigorous evaluative criteria remain.

The proposition that such anarchy necessarily follows from the decline in logical empiricism has withered under the scrutiny encouraged by authors such as Anderson (1986) in his description of the purposes and nature of critical relativism. However, many consumer researchers still shrink from the full implications of just what the implementation of postpositivistic methodologies might bring to the field (Calder & Tybout, 1987, 1989; Hunt, 1989; Muncy & Fisk, 1987). This lack of confidence receives partial justification from the fact that, with few exceptions, challengers to the neopositivist metaphysics have lacked specificity about how their research programs would actually progress. Those who have presented specific directions have sometimes implied that the researcher must make an a priori ideological commitment to one philosophical project (e.g., humanism) before undertaking research (Hirschman, 1986; Lincoln & Guba, 1985). This stance resembles the expectation that someone will undergo a conversion experience prior to receiving instruction in a new religious faith.

From these considerations, our present dual purpose unfolds. First, we present a continuum of philosophical concepts regarding the origin and content of knowledge relevant to consumer behavior phenomena. The end points of this epistemological continuum are Material Determinism (e.g., commonsense Empiricism) and Mental Determinism (e.g., pure Rationalism). Between these two extremes lie several philosophies varying in the relative degrees of Material versus Mental Determinism that they attribute to knowledge construction. For each epistemological position, we present the work of relevant philosophers and discuss their metaphysical assumptions.

Second, we present a set of research methods aimed at implementing inquiry from the viewpoint of each particular philosophical perspective. In outlining these approaches, we intend agreement with Anderson's (1986) position that "there are many alternative ways of constructing and justifying knowledge in the social sciences" (p. 158), the key requirement for validity entails a logical correspondence of the metaphysical assumptions made, on the one hand, with the aims, concepts, and methods employed, on the other. Toward the end of illustrating the role of such underlying assumptions, we shall explicate each approach via examples drawn from the literature in consumer research.

FROM DUALISM TO INTERACTIONISM AND COMMUNALISM

The origins of knowledge, together with its content and structure, raise questions that have long occupied the attention of philosophers (Langer, 1953; Mannheim, 1952; Polanyi & Prosch, 1975; Russell 1945). Although many proposed sources for knowledge exist, some clearly lie beyond our present concerns. These outlying sources include various mystical, spiritual, magical, or religious insights (Levine, 1985). While the content of these latter origins of knowledge and their effects on consumers and researchers may suggest worthwhile topics for scientific inquiry, they elude the possibility of direct human comprehension. Hence, we limit our discussion to knowledge deemed by

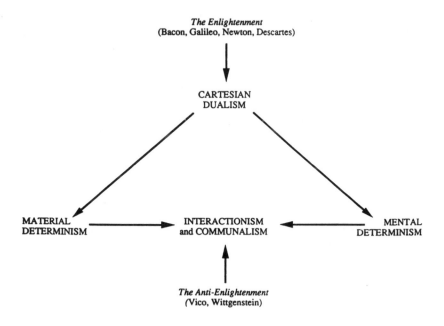

Figure 1.1. From Dualism to Interactionism and Communalism

the philosophy proposing it to originate from some natural and/or human source.

As indicated by the schematic diagram shown in Figure 1.1, two such natural origins have received by far the greatest share of attention: (a) the material world and (b) the human mind. Thus, Sperber (1985) observes that:

> If humans share specific attributes beyond anatomy, these must be the mental capacities which make possible the development of languages, cultures, and social systems. But what are these capacities? . . . For empiricists such as Locke, these capacities amount to an indefinite malleability and receptiveness, so that knowledge owes all its content and structure to experience and the environment. For rationalists such as Kant, human cognitive capacities comprise innate categories and principles which structure human knowledge and limit its variability. (p. 2)

Though this mind/matter distinction can be traced as far back as the difference between the Platonic Ideals and the Aristotelian Substances (Scruton, 1981), our narrative begins with Descartes and the Cartesian Dualism that arose from the split between body and soul—mind versus matter, the mental versus the physical, or subject versus object (Bernstein, 1983, p. 116; Rochberg-Halton, 1986, p. 134). In his *Meditations*, for example, Descartes (1986) started from the vantage point of radical skepticism, doubting everything, including the existence of his own body and the material world. He found that the only thing he could know with certainty was the existence of his own mind (the cogito or "I think"). From this, based on some shaky proofs for the existence of God, Descartes inferred the veridicality of his perceptions of the material world according to the conviction that an inherently perfect deity would not supply his creatures with false impressions (the argument that "God is no deceiver").

Besides emphasizing a mind/body problem that has since occupied modern philosophy (Campbell, 1984; Northrop, 1947), the Cartesian Dualism created a deep epistemological division between two extreme approaches to the problem of knowledge (Scruton, 1981). At one extreme, as indicated by our diagram, one might follow Descartes himself into a kind of Mental Determinism or Rationalism in which all knowledge originates in the operation of pure reason ("the natural light"). At the other extreme, as found in some aspects of Galileo and Newton (Northrop, 1947) or Bacon, Hobbes, and Locke (1974), one might subscribe to the Commonsense Empiricism of Material Determinism and hold that all knowledge stems from our direct experience of the material world via sense impressions that establish the contents of a "tabula rasa." However, as indicated by Scruton (1981), much of the development of modern philosophy has stemmed from internal tensions that have pushed these epistemological poles toward a rapprochement. This has taken the form of post-Kantian Interactionism in which things-in-themselves ("noumena") operate in conjunction with pre-existing mental concepts (the "categories") to form experiences ("phenomena") that reflect an interaction between mind and matter (Heritage, 1984, p. 39; Rochberg-Halton, 1986, p. 137; Scruton, 1982, pp. 18, 46).

> It is necessary to grasp Kant's important distinction between "phenomena" and "noumena." . . . Knowledge comes through the synthesis of concept and experience. . . . Phenomena . . . enter into causal relation with ourselves and our experience. (Scruton, 1981, p. 144)

Further, though Scruton (1982) challenges the clarity of Kant's (1929) demonstration that phenomenal experiences represent noumenal things-in-themselves, he allows that the latter position reached its fulfillment in the work of Wittgenstein (1958), who based his criterion of truth on the intersubjective use of language by a linguistic community (cf. Bruner, 1986, p. 132; Hawkes, 1977, p. 31; Sapir, 1949).

> In the . . . *Philosophical Investigations* Wittgenstein argues that there can be no knowledge of experience which does not presuppose reference to the public world. I can know my own experience . . . only because I apply to it concepts which gain their sense from public usage. And public usage describes a reality observable to others besides myself. The publicity of my language guarantees the objectivity of its reference. (Scruton, 1982, p. 35)

In other words, Wittgenstein's social theory of knowledge held that what a group considers to be reality exists as part of a language game governed by communal customs and involving the conventional character of meaning via concept applications in a shared public world (Bloor, 1983) without the possibility of a private language to describe individual sensations, inner experiences, or personal rules (Kripke, 1982). More recently, this postmodern perspective has been extended by such neo-pragmatists as Rorty, among others (1979, 1982).

As further indicated by our diagram, this Communalism reflects a second movement opposing the foundationism of the Enlightenment—that is, the search for an Archimedean Point to serve as the basis for Truth (as found in Descartes but also in Bacon or Newton)—against the tendency of a countervailing Anti-Enlightenment to ground knowledge in the social fabric of humanity (Hekman, 1986). For example, though he influenced few thinkers of his own day, Vico (1976) served the Anti-Enlightenment reaction by introducing a seminal break from the exaltation of reason and focusing instead on a view of human nature as rooted in the historical development of linguistic communities (Burke, 1985; Hawkes, 1977). From such foundations, extending not only through Wittgenstein (Bloor, 1983) but also through the work of the American pragmatists (James, Dewey, and especially Peirce), has emerged a language- and community-based emphasis on shared meanings with intersubjective truth criteria (Bernstein, 1983; Culler, 1975; Rochberg-Halton, 1986; Rorty, 1979, 1982; see also Feyerabend, 1975; Kuhn, 1970).

A CONTINUUM OF PHILOSOPHICAL POSITIONS

In sum, as suggested by our schematic representation shown in Table 1.1, Cartesian Dualism has evolved via the two partially separate routes of Interactionism and Communalism into what we may now characterize as a continuum of possible epistemological positions on the origins of knowledge. (For a continuum contrasting philosophies more germane to organizational behavior theory, see Morgan & Smircich, 1980.)

At one extreme, we find philosophies rooted in Material Determinism, such as Commonsense or Logical Empiricism which are associated with a Physical Construction of Reality, or PCR, and with a view of human nature as molded by sensory impressions or *homo sensans*.

At the other extreme we find epistemologies, such as Rationalism, that assume Mental Determinism of knowledge and the Mental Construction of Reality, or MCR, associated with *homo cogitans*.

In between lie intermediate philosophies of knowledge that contain some blend of, or some tension between, the two polar

TABLE 1.1

A Continuum of Philosophical Positions on the Origin of Knowledge

	Material Determinism		Interpretivism (Hermeneutics, Semiotics, Structural Criticism)	Subjectivism (Phenomenology, Existentialism)	Mental Determinism
Philosophy:	Empiricism (Commonsense Empiricism, Logical Empiricism)	Socioeconomic Constructionism (Marxism, Sociology of Knowledge, Ethnomethodology, Genetic Structuralism)	Interpretivism (Hermeneutics, Semiotics, Structural Criticism)	Subjectivism (Phenomenology, Existentialism)	Rationalism (Ideals, Innate Ideas, Archetypes)
View of Reality:	Physical Construction of Reality (PCR)	Social Construction of Reality (SCR)	Linguistic Construction of Reality (LCR)	Individual Construction of Reality (ICR)	Mental Construction of Reality (MCR)
View of Human Nature:	Homo Sensans	Homo Socius	Homo Narrans	Homo Individuus	Homo Cogitans
Representative Scholars:	Locke, Berkeley, Hume, Ayer, Hempel, Popper	Marx, Engels, Mannheim, Schutz, Garfinkel, Goldmann	Schleiermacher, Dilthy	Sartre, Heidegger, Husserl	Plato, Leibniz, Spinoza, Fichte-Kant, Jung

NOTE: Our names for the various views of human nature come from the following sources: Homo Socius (Berger & Luckmann, 1966, p. 51); Homo Narrans (Fisher, 1985); Homo Individuus (by analogy with Homo Socius); Homo Cogitans (Bruner, 1986, p. 41).

perspectives. Arrayed in order of their relative balance of material/ mental determinism (Mind versus Matter), these include: Socio-economic Constructionism (the Social Construction of Reality or SCR; *homo socius*); Interpretivism (the Linguistic Construction of Reality or LCR; *homo narrans*); and Subjectivism (the Individual Construction of Reality or ICR; *homo individuus*).

Table 1.1 also illustrates each perspective along the continuum with various specific philosophical approaches (shown parenthetically at the top) and various representative scholars (listed at the bottom).

Although other epistemological orientations might have been chosen (e.g., Behaviorism instead of Marxism or Narratology instead of Hermeneutics),[1] the selected approaches appear useful for two reasons. First, they relate closely to the research methodologies discussed later. Second, they bear a clear relevance to phenomena that are of interest to consumer-behavior researchers. With these premises in mind, we shall now turn to brief examinations of the principal tenets underlying the competing epistemologies. To provide maximum clarity, in Part I (Chapters 2 through 6), we shall move from left to right in Table 1.1, tracing the continuum that lies between Material and Mental Determinism.

NOTE

1. As one reviewer, Julie Ozanne, has noted: "If these approaches, for instance, were structured in two-dimensional space with the vertical axis being change vs. order, Phenomenology and Existentialism would be positioned in opposition, as would Marxism and Sociology of Knowledge. Phenomenology and Sociology of Knowledge both focus on preserving the existing social order, while Existentialism and Marxism both stress change" (personal communication). (For an extended discussion on this topic see Burrell, Gibson, and Morgan [1979], *Sociological Paradigms and Organizational Analysis*. London: Heinemann.)

➤ PART ONE ◄

THE PHILOSOPHIES

2

EMPIRICISM

COMMONSENSE EMPIRICISM

In its commonsense version typical of Bacon and Hobbes (Northrop, 1947; Scruton, 1981) and even in its early systematic formulation by Locke (1974), traditional empiricism held that experiences, taken by empiricists as the foundation of all knowledge, had their ultimate origins in the sensations coming from the "powers" and "primary qualities," such as shape and movement, in the external world of physical matter. For Locke (1974), these primary qualities and powers produced directly corresponding ideas of primary qualities as well as certain secondary qualities (such as color and smell). However, this seemingly innocent admission that sensations produce ideas that contain some secondary qualities not directly linked to corresponding primary qualities in the physical world ultimately drove a wedge between experience and material reality from which Empiricism could not quickly or easily recover (Scruton, 1981).

Hume (1974) pushed the logic of empiricism to its skeptical limits by showing that our experience gives us no adequate grounds for establishing necessity in causality (e.g., we have no clear perception of the necessary connection between cause and effect). So, all our assumptions concerning causal relationships, including the conviction that external objects prompt internal experiences, depend on nothing more secure than the force of habit in observing constant conjunctions (which have no logical force in establishing causal connections). In other words, via the problem of induction, constant conjunctions of events found in the past are logically consistent with virtually any prediction concerning virtually any future state of affairs. In short, Hume's skepticism systematically stripped away any logical grounds that we might take as adequate justification for believing that our internal experiences reflect physical properties of an external material world.

LOGICAL EMPIRICISM

Yet, as Ayer (1980) has shown, one can read Hume as holding out some hope for the commonsense view that a factual world of material reality exists and that we accurately perceive it. The basis for this hope lies in Hume's emphasis on the role of habit, custom, or expectations and his conviction that human nature is constituted in a manner that leads us toward accepting this type of evidence (p. 71). Though Ayer himself rejects such a course, this path toward trying to sidestep the problem of induction leads toward Falsificationism (Popper 1959) and provides some support for the neopositivistic doctrines strongly held by many consumer-behavior researchers even today (e.g., Calder & Tybout, 1987, 1989).

Within the social sciences, the logical empiricist tradition has embraced the metaphysical assumptions that

> the social world is a hard, concrete, real thing "out there," which affects everyone. . . . It can be thought of as a structure composed

of a network of determinate relationships between constituent parts. Reality is to be found in the concrete behavior and relationships between these parts. It is an objective phenomenon that lends itself to accurate observation and measurement. . . . Reality by definition is that which is external and real. The social world is as concrete and real as the natural world. (Morgan & Smircich, 1980, p. 495)

This view depicts humans as

a product of the external forces in the environment to which they have been exposed. Stimuli in their environment condition them to behave and respond to events in predictable and determinate ways. A network of causal relationships links all important aspects of behavior to context. Though human perception may influence this process to some degree, people always respond to situations in a lawful (i.e., rule-governed) manner (Morgan & Smircich, 1980, p. 495)

More broadly, as illustrated in an earlier treatise by Ayer (1956), an emphasis on the role of experience in providing empirical evidence corresponds to the general hypothetico-deductive method espoused by such philosophers of science as Hempel (1966) and widely adopted by the consumer-behavior mainstream (e.g., Hunt, 1983). In this light, one can use Logical Empiricism to justify the Physical Construction of Reality or PCR as follows:

The reason why our sense-experiences afford us grounds for believing in the existence of physical objects is simply that sentences which are taken as referring to physical objects are used in such a way that our having the appropriate experiences counts in favour of their truth. It is characteristic of what is meant by such a sentence as "there is a cigarette case on this table" that my having just the experience that I am having is evidence for the truth of the statement which it expresses. . . . For if such a statement functions as part of a theory which accounts for our experiences, it must be possible for them to justify it. (Ayer, 1956, pp. 132-133)

The logical empiricist view seeks to ground knowledge in the external world, which is deemed immutable. Its appeals to verification and truth are, therefore, based on the accumulation of "brute data."

> The basic building block of knowledge on this view is the impression, or sense-datum. . . . The highest ambition would be to build our knowledge from such building blocks by judgements which could be anchored in a certainty beyond subjective intuition. . . . Verification must be grounded ultimately in the acquisition of brute data . . . data whose validity cannot be questioned by offering another interpretation or reading. (Taylor, 1985, p. 19)

The logical empiricist searches for an objective anchor or Archimedean point on which knowledge may be unequivocally constructed (Bernstein, 1985). The desire is for certainty, consistency, and the progressive elimination of ambiguity.

SUGGESTED READING

Ayer, A. J. (1980). *Hume.* New York: Hill and Wang.

Morgan, G. & Smircich, L. (1980). The case for qualitative research, *Academy of Management Review, 5*, 4, 491-500.

Scruton, R. (1981). *From Descartes to Wittgenstein.* New York: Harper & Row.

3

SOCIOECONOMIC CONSTRUCTIONISM

F rom philosophies that are grounded in the external reality of an immutable world, we move to those based on determinate social realities. Within the overall category of Socioeconomic Constructionism, as indicated by Table 1.1, we shall emphasize the philosophies of Marxism, the Mannheimian sociology of knowledge, the ethnomethodology of Schutz and Garfinkel, and Goldmann's genetic structuralism. The epistemologies included here share a tendency to attribute the origin of knowledge to social and/or economic sources.

> Human thought is consummately social: social in its origins, social in its functions, social in its forms, social in its applications. (Geertz, 1973, p. 360)

MARXISM

Undoubtedly, the most celebrated, and condemned, philosophy of Socioeconomic Constructionism was proposed by Marx
(1970, 1973; Marx & Engels, 1968, 1978). Because of socialism's
political implications, with rare exceptions such as Firat and
Dholakia, American consumer-behavior scholars have usually
hesitated to base their research on Marxist philosophy and may
even lack any well developed understanding of its principal
tenets. This neglect seems unfortunate because, once one tames
one's preconceptions and steps back from the political arena,
basic Marxist philosophy appears neither especially disturbing
nor even counterintuitive.

One problem immediately encountered in discussing Marxist
philosophy arises from its widely varying interpretations. Indeed, over time, Marx himself lapsed into various inconsisten-
cies (Althusser, 1971, 1972a, 1972b). For example, consider the
notion of *ideology*, clearly a central concept of Marxist thought:

> Even within the Marxist tradition there are controversies about
> what Marx actually meant, about what the implications of the
> Marxist theory of ideology are, and about a variety of epistemo-
> logical, sociological, and other issues which flow from this theory.
> (Wolff, 1981, p. 50)

Despite such variations, one finds a strong tendency in Marxist literature toward the notion "that the ideas and beliefs
people have are systematically related to their actual and material conditions of existence" (Wolff, 1981, p. 50; see also Kurzweil
1980, p. 234; Scruton, 1981, p. 222). Hence,

> in terms of the sociology of knowledge, this is a deep change in
> the evolution of the discipline. More than any other post-Enlight-
> enment thinker, Marx established the basic principle of the sociology
> of knowledge: all thought is socially and historically determined.
> (Hekman, 1986, p. 22)

This fundamental proposition concerning the Social Construction of Reality (SCR) can, of course, appear in more politically charged language (e.g., Hawthorne, 1977, p. 217). However, when stripped of its potentially inflammatory rhetoric, Marxism can also provide a constructive viewpoint on how meanings arise from material objects in the social world. This descriptive aspect of the Marxist SCR informs the semiotic approach of Eco (1976).

> In the first book of Das Kapital, Marx not only shows how all commodities, in a general exchange system, can become signs standing for other commodities: he also suggests that this relation of mutual significance is made possible because the commodities system is structured by means of opposition. . . . This signifying relationship is made possible by the cultural existence of an exchange parameter [termed] exchange value. . . . In an exchange system, exchange value refers back to the quantity of human labor necessary to the production of Commodity 1 and Commodity 2. All these items can be correlated . . . with the universal equivalent, money. (p. 25)

Thus, in accord with SCR, Marxism proposes the origin of knowledge in the social relations of economic production activities. Human thought and consciousness reflect socioeconomic activity; hence, all meaning stems from one's activities in the economic, social world (Wolff, 1981).

Beyond stressing Socioeconomic Constructionism as the basis for meaning, Marxism makes additional proposals relevant to technologically advanced societies. Some of these concern the role of *false consciousness*. Specifically, Marxism proposes that within simple economies (with undifferentiated manual labor), all workers will possess the same "correct," materially based ideology or consciousness, due to their identical relationships to the process of production. For Marx, all such knowledge coming directly from manual production activities is "true" or "honest."

By contrast, in complex differentiated economies, a portion of the population will work as thinkers and intellectuals, thereby losing their direct connection to manual activity and knowledge. Once the relationship between material production and meaning has broken down, inappropriate systems of thought arise. Such inappropriate consciousness would include those of the *ruling class*—the economic elite, which is removed from manual production. Their incorrect system of consciousness, according to Marx, is promulgated through their control of cultural institutions, such as communications media and government. (For a useful introduction to the manner in which this insight gives rise to a politically oriented critical theory directed toward the unmasking of ideology and not directly concerned with the theme of the present work, see Rogers 1987.) To Marx, when people ceased to be in direct productive contact with their material surroundings, they lost contact with themselves and fell victim to abusers of economic or political power. To escape such exploitation, the populace must return to the true meanings acquired from direct, manual experience with the material world and must reject forms of consciousness originating elsewhere (Wolff, 1975, p. 39).

MANNHEIM'S SOCIOLOGY OF KNOWLEDGE

In the context of consumer behavior, one shortcoming of Marxist philosophy concerns its assumption of a single prevailing cultural ideology as the basis for SCR via either a "correct" or "false" consciousness. By contrast, while consumer-behavior theory generally accepts the existence of overarching cultural milieus (e.g., the French culture or the German market), it also recognizes the existence of many subcultural differences based on race, nationality, and religion. Hence, neo-Marxist theorists have extended the concept of ideology to include alternative meaning systems within different subcultural ideologies (Williams, 1965, 1973, 1977, 1979).

As a founder of the sociology of knowledge, Mannheim identified and described the differences in knowledge structures among various social groupings. In *Ideology and Utopia* (1936), Mannheim stated that:

> Two persons, carrying on a discussion in the same universe of discourse—corresponding to the same historical-social conditions—can and must do so quite differently from two persons identified with different social positions. . . . Ours is a world in which social groupings, which had hitherto lived more or less isolated from one another, are now merging into one another. Not only the various nations . . . but also the various social strata of these nations, which previously had been more or less self-contained, and finally the various occupational groups within these strata and the intellectual groups in this most highly differentiated world—all are now thrown out of the self-sufficient, complacent state of taking themselves for granted, and are forced to maintain themselves and their ideas in the face of the onslaught of these heterogeneous groups. (pp. 279-280)

Knowledge structures differ across these various social groupings, Mannheim proposes, because the socioeconomic conditions of their existence differ. Hence, like Marx, he views social production activity as the source for all human knowledge, but recognizes, as Marxists generally do not, that complex societies include many possible "social realities." The SCRs available to ethnic minorities, women, migrant farm workers, or persons who grew up during the Depression will differ not only from one another but also from those available to whites, men, investment bankers, or baby boomers. Thus, individual worldviews or *Weltanschauungen* will vary systematically across genders, races, occupations, and generations (Mannheim, 1952). As Mannheim notes, "the vain hope of discovering truth in a form which is independent of a historically and socially determined set of meanings will have to be given up" (p. 71).

Mannheim's thesis suggests that meaning is relative to the social experience of the individual and thereby entails the concepts of relativism and perspectivism. Indeed, within SCR, relativism inevitably results from systematic variations in the points of contact between people from different social groupings, each developing its own distinct ideology to reflect its unique perspective on society. This form of relativism is therefore also termed *perspectivism* (Wolff, 1975, p. 39). Muncy and Fisk (1987) refer to a form of perspectivism based solely on occupational grouping as "objective relativism."

For Mannheim, the presence of heterogeneous perspectivism in complex societies encourages the disintegration of communication processes. Diverse social groupings fail to communicate because their different experiential perspectives assign different meanings to the same material objects. Mannheim's proposals have obvious relevance for marketers who must communicate effectively with diverse market segments, each of which may ascribe a different meaning to the product. A similar phenomenon characterizes the miscommunication often found among the disparate social sciences. Various disciplines have assigned different meanings to the same social phenomenon (e.g., social class, institution, attitude, motive) and even to the same word (e.g., "image," "symbol," "sex"), with the result that researchers frequently "talk past one another" (Mannheim 1936, p. 281).

Despite such communication problems, however, Mannheim remained optimistic that differences in perspectives on what constitutes truth and meaning could be at least partially overcome through a process of rapprochement.

> A total view implies both the *assimilation and transcendence* of the limitations of particular points of view. It represents the continuous process of the expansion of knowledge, and has as its goal not achievement of a super-temporally valid conclusion but the broadest extension of our horizon of vision. (pp. 94-95)

Here, Mannheim's vision resembles that of Gadamer's hermeneutic fusion of horizons, a doctrine we shall discuss at length in a subsequent section.

ETHNOMETHODOLOGY

Like Marxism and Mannheim's construal of the sociology of knowledge, ethnomethodology addresses the cultural level, where it focuses on the stock of *commonsense knowledge* present in a society and seeks to ascertain its rules and principles. Thus, ethnomethodology aims to discover what people believe they know—that is, what constructs and schemas they view as objective and factual—and by what social processes they come to think they know these things (Leiter, 1980, p. 1).

As one of the two principal intellectual forces behind ethnomethodology, Alfred Schutz (1964) supplied the bulk of its philosophical apparatus, including the concepts of "the stock of knowledge at hand" and the "natural attitude of everyday life." The stock of knowledge at hand contains two types of SCR: (a) recipes, rules of thumb, and maxims (roughly comparable to contingent scripts) and (b) social types or categorizations of people, objects, and events (roughly comparable to idealized prototypes).

With regard to the stock of knowledge, Schutz proposes (a) that the bulk of personal knowledge is acquired through socialization (e.g., from teachers, parents, books, the mass media, etc.), (b) that certain groups possess specialized knowledge not known to others, (c) that, if needed, people will seek specialized knowledge from others, and (d) that the stock of knowledge possessed by any one individual becomes highly developed where useful in a practical way, but remains undeveloped and sketchy where not required for the day-to-day affairs of life.

> Clear and distinct experiences are intermingled with vague conjectures; suppositions and prejudices cross well-proven evidences; motives, means and ends, as well as causes and effects are strung together without clear understanding of their real connections. There are everywhere gaps, intermissions, discontinuities. (Schutz, 1964, pp. 72-73)

Meanwhile, in Schutz's version of SCR, the natural attitude of everyday life is experienced as an ongoing social world that existed before we were born and will continue to exist after we die. Further, people also assume that others in the same culture share the same belief system and, therefore, the same experience of the world (Berger & Luckmann, 1966; Schutz & Luckmann, 1974).

As the second great force behind ethnomethodology, Garfinkel (1967) extended Schutz's philosophical notions by applying them empirically to sociological phenomena and by comparing them explicitly with the assumptions of scientific rationality. Garfinkel argued that commonsense knowledge is not just an inferior version of scientific knowledge, but rather is substantively different in its rationalities and applications. In particular, Garfinkel (1967) explored how commonsense knowledge shared by participants in an interaction creates and sustains the apparently objective and factual nature of the social world.

One facet of Garfinkel's (1967) perspective that has particular relevance to consumer researchers concerns his emphasis on the practical reasoning by which participants infer such social rules as those that govern consumption behavior within some community of understanding. Through a series of ingenious experiments and case studies, Garfinkel focused on uncovering the structures of expectations that govern the SCR of everyday life. For example, he examines the case of "Agnes," a 19-year-old transsexual "whose female measurements of 38-25-38 were accompanied by a fully developed penis and scrotum" (p. 117). Here, Agnes attracts interest primarily for the manner in which she drew upon consumption-related norms and roles successfully to establish her preferred sexual identity as a female. In attempting to pass for a woman, she had to learn such "rules of the game as what clothes to wear, how to cook, and how to practice such stereotypically feminine skills as sewing and shopping" (p. 146). Agnes' transsexuality helps make those of us who have always consumed according to the gender rules associated with our natural sex aware that gender consumption patterns are a learned, socially constructed set of norms. In sum, as a "practical methodologist" studying and manipulating the consumption-oriented props of everyday social life, "Agnes was well aware of the devices that she used to make visible the constancy of the valuable, self-same, natural, normal female" (p. 183). Hence, the experience of Agnes serves as a special case of Garfinkel's dictum that

> Socially-sanctioned-facts-of-life-in-society-that-any-bona-fide-member-of-the-society-knows depict such matters as the conduct of . . . market organization. (p. 76)

In sum, ethnomethodology implicitly assumes the existence of a socially constructed reality in which all persons participate. Though people may have somewhat differing perspectives within this socially constructed reality,

> in their communications, members assume that if they were to change places, each would see what the other sees from his perspective. Members also assume that while they are biographically unique, the experiences of each are sufficiently congruent to permit them to ignore any differences that might be due to personal experiences and perceptions "until further notice." Further, when discrepancies do arise, the presumed underlying congruence permits them to *use those differences* as a scheme of interpretation for understanding each other. (Leiter, 1980, p. 174)

Thus, in ethnomethodology, people are assumed to share a sufficiently common SCR to interpolate between disparate personal perspectives. In this worldview, "our similarities outweigh our differences."

GENETIC STRUCTURALISM

Lucien Goldmann (1964, 1967a, 1967b, 1969, 1975) adapted the influences of the Marxist philosopher Georg Lukacs (1963, 1965, 1971, 1974) and the structuralist Lévi-Strauss (1978) to develop a view of SCR that he referred to as genetic structuralism. Goldmann's view holds that cultural products serve as the expression of a cohesive social group and therein follows Marx,

Mannheim, and Garfinkel in attributing SCR to social/material conditions that shape a collective consciousness within the group (Kurzweil, 1980, p. 187; Wolff, 1981, p. 57). The Marxist orientation suggests that the formation of a collective consciousness will occur most frequently within social classes (Goldmann, 1969, pp. 101-102). However, other social divisions within a national culture (e.g., race, religion, and perhaps even occupation) will also produce distinctive forms of collective consciousness, or worldviews, among group members.

A key difference between Goldmann's genetic structuralism and the approaches of Marx, Mannheim, and Garfinkel concerns Goldmann's push toward inferring the *Weltanschauung* of a social group from an examination of its cultural products. Thus, while Marx, Mannheim, and Garfinkel describe the transfer of knowledge from the social world to conscious thought, Goldmann proposes that the collective consciousness of the group will, in turn, appear in the artifacts it creates. Hence, to understand a group's collective consciousness, we must examine the content and structure of meaning embedded within its material and intellectual culture. In his role as a literary critic, for example, Goldmann (1967a, b) provides several insightful readings of the *Pensees of Pascal* to reconstruct the worldviews of the French social classes during the seventeenth century (Outhwaite, 1975, p. 73).

Another aspect of Goldmann's philosophy relevant to consumer-behavior theory posits the existence in every culture of what he terms the *exceptional individual* (Goldmann, 1964, p. 18; 1969b, p. 346). These are persons who have absorbed all or most of a particular social group's worldview and then turn their creative abilities toward translating that worldview into cultural objects. Such cultural objects thereby become modes of communicative expression permitting members of other social groups to view the collective consciousness of the group represented by the author. Possible examples of the exceptional individual in our own culture might include Spike Lee's portrayal of African-American consciousness in *Do the Right Thing;* Steven Spielberg's evocation of the fantasies of white, middle-class children in *E.T.: The Extraterrestrial;* the many songs by David Frishberg that evoke the consciousness of the aging, nostalgia-prone sports fan; and Elie Wiesel's essays depicting the worldview of Holocaust survivors. In such instances,

> the writer's consciousness coincides with the world vision of his group, so that more or less identical structures will be found in his work and in the world vision itself, and in the social situation which gave rise to both of these. . . . This is the essence of Goldmann's [philosophy], then; a homology of social structure and literary creation, mediated by the world vision. (Wolff 1975, pp. 85-86)

SUGGESTED READING

Leiter, K. C. (1980). *A primer on ethnomethodology.* New York: Oxford University Press.

Mannheim, K. (1952). *Essays on the sociology of knowledge.* London: Routledge.

Wolff, J. (1981). *Hermeneutic philosophy and the sociology of art.* London: Routledge and Kegan Paul.

Wolff, J. (1981). *The social production of art.* New York: St. Martin's.

4

INTERPRETIVISM

Clearly, Goldmann's version of SCR moves us some distance in the direction of Interpretivism or, in this chapter, what we shall call the Linguistic Construction of Reality (LCR). Recently, thanks to work by Hudson and Ozanne (1988) on alternative ways of knowing, by O'Shaughnessy (1987) on hermeneutics, and by Mick (1986) on semiotics, this general perspective has gained greater currency among consumer researchers. Therefore, as indicated in Table 1.1, we shall confine our comments to some relatively brief summary remarks on hermeneutics, semiotics, and their application via structural criticism.

HERMENEUTICS

As a field of study, hermeneutics emerged from the age-old efforts by classical and biblical scholars to interpret the meanings of texts such as those found in Greek literature and the Old

Testament. (For historical and critical reviews, see Bleicher, 1980 and Thompson, 1981.) Such interpretive projects inevitably raise questions of validity and pose problems in developing sound hermeneutic methods. These issues received an early systematic formulation in the work of Schleiermacher (1978), who viewed interpretation as directed at the recovery of the author's intended meaning and who introduced the concept of the *Hermeneutic Circle* as involving (a) a movement back and forth between an essentially divinatory (intuitive) and comparative (classificatory) grasp of the overall sense in a passage of text and (b) a systematic justification of this overview via psychological and grammatical interpretations of the passage's components.

Dilthey (1972) further developed this sense of the circular process by which an interpretation of the whole text guides the exegesis of its parts, which, in turn, shape an understanding of the whole (Makkreel, 1975). To this emphasis on hermeneutic circularity, Dilthey added a distinction between natural sciences, *Naturwissenschaften*, and human studies, *Geisteswissenschaften*. Dilthey's contrast viewed the projects of studying nature versus human society as two very different sorts of endeavors—the first more consistent with the objectives of the Enlightenment (Bacon, Newton, et al.) and the second more in tune with the social/historical/linguistic focus of the Anti-Enlightenment (i.e., Vico and his successors such as Rousseau and Nietzsche). (For good reviews of this tension between systems of thought, see Bleicher, 1982; Hekman, 1986; Thompson, 1981.)

Hence, for anyone wishing to claim that Interpretivism is "scientific" in the generally accepted (neopositivistic) sense of that term, the Hermeneutic Circle and the distinction between the natural sciences and human studies remains a source of potential embarrassment—an embarrassment encouraging moves toward either evasion or repair.

Drawing on the work of Heidegger (1962), particularly Heidegger's treatment of "foreunderstanding," or preconceptions, in phenomenological experience (a concept clearly related to Kant's treatment of innate mental categories), Hans

Georg Gadamer (1975) attempted to build a cogent justification for the role of the Hermeneutic Circle in the process of interpreting a text. Specifically, he examined the role of "prejudices," that is, prejudgments, foreunderstandings, or preconceptions, in guiding an explication of the parts that, in turn, modify one's understanding of the whole via a self-corrective cycle reminiscent of a cybernetic feedback loop. Via this process of self-correction, the Hermeneutic Circle moves toward what Gadamer (1975) called *a fusion of horizons* by which the interpreter's perspective (including his or her admittedly "prejudicial" view of the whole text) merges with the worldview of the textual tradition (including the role of the author's intentions and their interplay with the interpretive community). As explained by Habermas (1971), "the elastic procedure of hermeneutic anticipations . . . with their circular corroboration" leads toward "the hermeneutic procedure of continually correcting one's preunderstanding on the basis of the text" (p. 259). Further, by Gadamer's argument, all interpretive activity, including that found in the natural sciences, involves this kind of circular self-corrective interplay between the whole and its parts (the theory and its supporting data).

> Gadamer provides an ontological explanation of human existence that reveals the universality and linguisticality of hermeneutic understanding. . . . Such a method would reject the Enlightenment search for truth and objectivity, accept the role of prejudice in the universal phenomenon of human understanding, and define interpretation in terms of the fusion of horizons and effective-historical consciousness. (Hekman, 1986, p. 156)

This recognition helps to prepare the way for a postpositivistic or postmodern reassessment of scientific method in the social sciences (e.g., Lincoln & Guba, 1985). (For an excellent review in the context of marketing and consumer research, see Sherry, 1991.)

Ricoeur (1976, 1981) carried Gadamer's justification of the Hermeneutic Circle even farther by following Hirsch (1967) in drawing clear parallels between the process of interpreting a text and Popper's (1959) falsificationism. Though insisting, in opposition to Hirsch, that the interpretation of a text properly aims for the recovery of multivocal or plurivocal meanings, rather than any univocal intention of its author, Ricoeur (1976) joins Hirsch in arguing that interpretive validity rests on a falsificationistic enterprise wherein one forms a tentative interpretation of the whole (an hypothesis) and then tests this overview against a close reading of the parts (the evidence), adjusting the broader interpretation (revising the theory) as needed to correct it for discrepancies with the more detailed textual content (the data). Further, Ricoeur (1976) embraces a second aspect of hermeneutic analysis: namely, that provided by the more technically oriented tools of semiotics.

SEMIOTICS

Semiotics, the study of signs, grew from independent but apposite contributions by the Swiss linguist Ferdinand de Saussure (1959) and the American Pragmatist Charles S. Peirce (1955). (For good general reviews, see Barthes, 1967; Eco, 1976; Guiraud, 1975; Sebeok, 1981. For more specific reviews, anchored in the context of consumer research, see Mick, 1986, 1988.) These thinkers adopted somewhat different terminologies (e.g., "semiological" versus "semiotic") and constructed partially contrasting views of the sign process as a two-way Saussurean interaction between a signifier and a signified versus a three-way Peircean relation between a sign, a designatum, and an interpretant (with a rough equivalence between Saussure's signifier/signified and Peirce's sign/interpretant). However, most importantly for our present purposes, both perspectives converge on the crucial role played by signs of all types (words, pictures, music, objects, products) in shaping the meaning of people's lives (Mick, 1986).

One facet of Peirce's influence—most notably via his student Charles Morris (1946, 1964)—moved in the direction of positivistic aspects of the semiotic perspective. Specifically, Morris (1964) regarded the interpretant as a type of behavior to be measured by such techniques as the Semantic Differential (Osgood, Suci, & Tannenbaum, 1957). This positivistic thrust prepared the way for laboratory studies (Morris, 1964) that anticipated related aspects of experimental esthetics (e.g., Berlyne, 1971, 1974). Much of the work on consumer esthetics in consumer-behavior research has drawn on this perspective in its attempt to test the effects of artistic features on appreciative responses. (For a recent review, see Holbrook, 1987.)

By contrast, one facet of Saussure's linguistic emphasis led to a focus on the structure of *binary oppositions* as a key to the recovery of meaning (e.g., Lévi-Strauss 1968a & b, 1978; Scholes, 1974, 1982). This structuralist focus on homologies among differences or contrasts suggests a more qualitative text-centered type of analysis that aligns closely with the previously stated objectives of Interpretivism. Here, the project involves a structuring of textual evidence in a manner that supports a general reading of its meaning. As Peirce himself pointed out, this interpretive approach proceeds by abduction (inferring the nature of a case from the conjunction of a general rule or theory and a more specific textual item or result) rather than by the more positivistic logic of deduction or induction. Importantly, Peirce acknowledges the presence of researcher preconceptions in structuring the abduction process. Without such preconceptions, the researcher would have no basis upon which to generate an initial inquiry. Thus, the interpretive task is not to remove such preconceptions, but rather to test them critically during the course of the analysis. (For a detailed treatment of abduction, see Eco & Sebeok, 1983; for discussions within the context of consumer-behavior and consumer research, see Holbrook, 1987 and Mick, 1986.)

Hence, Peirce's abduction provides a justification for the validity of Interpretivism quite similar to that provided by the previously mentioned arguments on behalf of the Hermeneutic Circle. Pursuing this general orientation toward the Linguistic Construction of Reality (LCR), Holbrook (1987) has recently argued for the greater use of interpretive, as opposed to neo-positivistic, semiology in the study of consumption and consumer-behavior phenomena. One route toward that objective lies in the techniques developed in the application of structural criticism (Lévi-Strauss, 1963, 1978; Ricoeur, 1976).

STRUCTURAL CRITICISM

As described later in more detail, the structuralist's critical stance applies LCR by viewing the semiotics of any symbolic system, including the consumption of everyday products or other common aspects of the human condition, as a text (e.g., Farrell, 1985; Fisher, 1985; Ricoeur, 1981) that shapes its own hermeneutic interpretation via a series of binary oppositions, differences, or contrasts (Barthes, 1967; Guiraud, 1975; Lévi-Strauss, 1963, 1978; Scholes, 1974, 1982). Famous examples include Propp's (1968) analysis of Russian folk tales, Lévi-Strauss's (1963) explication of the Oedipus myth, and Barthes' (1983) exegesis of the fashion system. In literary circles, this approach to LCR appears in Barthes' (1974) tome-length examination of one short story by Balzac. For illustrations more accessible to an American audience, one might study the examples provided by Scholes (1974, 1982).

All such specific instances rely heavily on detailed, lengthy, close readings of the text in question (whether it be a literary work or some other aspect of the symbolic culture) and, there-fore, suffer from any attempt at summary, abbreviation, or condensation. To avoid this pitfall, we shall simply point the reader to the literature representing this mode of analysis with the strong suggestion that it contains perspectives and insights well worth exploring within the context of consumption sym-bolism, consumer-behavior imagery, and business-related signs (Culler, 1975; Scholes, 1974, 1982; Sturrock, 1979). (For recent examples relevant to consumer research, see Holbrook & Hirschman, 1992.)

SUGGESTED READING

Bleicher, J. (1982). *The hermeneutic imagination: Outline of a positive critique of scientism and sociology.* London: Routledge and Kegan Paul.

Hekman, S. J. (1986). *Hermeneutics and the sociology of knowledge.* Notre Dame, IL: University of Notre Dame Press.

Scholes, R. (1982). *Semiotics and interpretation.* New Haven, CT: Yale University Press.

Thompson, J. B. (1981). *Critical hermeneutics.* Cambridge: Cambridge University Press.

5

SUBJECTIVISM

Two prominent subjectivist philosophies, phenomenology and existentialism, emerged in the early 1900s—a time when social catastrophes fostered ideologies such as nihilism or anarchism and when sociopsychological vocabularies embraced concepts like anomie or crisis of identity. As shown in Table 1.1, the emerging subjectivist philosophies focused primarily on the discovery and validation of self-knowledge— an intellectual task whose urgency increased as the world appeared ever more likely to disintegrate—giving rise to a view of humanity that we might characterize as *homo individuus*.

PHENOMENOLOGY

Stated in its simplest form, phenomenological philosophy, as opposed to the more broadly conceived psychological phenomenology, attempts to comprehend how the individual interacts with external objects to achieve knowledge structures that compose an

Individual Construction of Reality or ICR (Wolff, 1975, p. 6; Thompson, Locander, & Pollio, 1989). Phenomenological meaning differs in two important respects from that of the philosophies previously discussed in Chapters 2 through 4. First, it adopts a primarily psychological focus on the individual rather than on the social group, subculture, or culture. Second, it reflects a further shift in the relative balance between Material Determinism and Mental Determinism by assuming a greater predominance of the latter as a basis for knowledge. In short, phenomenology holds that, after being co-constituted by the interaction between an individual's consciousness and the social world, ICR resides primarily in the mind. In this, phenomenology shares insights in common with certain philosophies of the East:

> What must be grasped is the fundamental insight of the Orient that the immediately apprehended is quite other than the scientifically, philosophically and theologically postulated and yet is nevertheless an ultimate and essential component of reality worthy of attention and contemplation in and for itself. (Northrop, 1947, p. 391)

As the seminal phenomenological thinker, Edmund Husserl (1960) proposed a novel approach to knowledge centered in the "certainty of conscious thought" (Eagleton, 1983, p. 54). Like Descartes, he began the search for meaning by rejecting the realistic, empirical, commonsense of Material Determinism (i.e., that we correctly perceive an external world of physical objects). Instead, Husserl found his epistemological anchor in the way that objects appear to us in our conscious thought. Following Brentano, he regarded such "intentional objects" not as things in themselves, but as phenomena of consciousness, arguing that all consciousness is consciousness *of* something and that all thought points toward the consideration of some phenomenon. Hence, to grasp knowledge with certainty, we must bracket the external world by focusing only on the contents of consciousness. This *phenomenological reduction* provides the only reliable data we possess (Eagleton, 1983, p. 55).

We put out of action the general thesis which belongs to the essence of the natural standpoint, we place in brackets whatever it includes respecting the nature of Being: this entire natural world . . . is a "fact-world" of which we continue to be conscious, even though it pleases us to put it in brackets. (Husserl, 1931)

A final aspect of Husserl's ICR involves the concept of pure phenomenological essences. In the phenomena of consciousness, Husserl posited, such essences (i.e., the attributes or characteristics most central to an object) could be examined in their pure or ideal form to create a certain or accurate understanding of the object itself. In this, Husserl revived the earlier Platonic conception of pure Forms or Ideas and the medieval doctrine of common nature or essence, which has been known as *essentialism* (Seung, 1982).

[Phenomena] are a system of universal essences, for phenomenology varies each object in imagination until it discovers what is invariable about it. What is presented to phenomenological knowledge is not just, say, the colour red, but the universal essence of this thing, redness as such. To grasp any phenomenon wholly and purely is to grasp what is essential and unchanging about it. (Eagleton, 1983, p. 55)

EXISTENTIALISM

In discussing *existentialism*, a term coined by Kierkegaard (Scruton, 1981, p. 187), we shall concentrate primarily on the philosophies of Martin Heidegger and Jean-Paul Sartre. As a student of Husserl, Heidegger's intellectual genesis lay in phenomenological philosophy. However, he broke from this tradition by rejecting the transcendence of consciousness (via the aforementioned pure essences). Instead, for Heidegger, knowledge originated in the *Gestalt* or totality of human existence. He referred to this existential *Gestalt* as *Dasein* (i.e., "being there"). As Eagleton (1983) notes, "to move from Husserl to Heidegger is to move from the terrain of pure intellect to a philosophy which meditates on what it feels like to be alive" (p. 62).

For Heidegger, the most fundamental basis for knowledge was existence itself. To comprehend one's existence in the world (i.e., *Dasein*) was to achieve self-understanding. This self-understanding could then be directed outward toward comprehending the meaning of other entities.

> Dasein is an entity which does not just occur among other entities. . . . It is peculiar to this entity that with and through its Being, this Being is disclosed to it. Understanding of Being is itself the defining characteristic of Dasein's Being. (Heidegger, 1962, p. 32)

Importantly for our later discussion of existential methodology, Heidegger suggests an essentially hermeneutical approach for moving one's comprehension of existence outward from the self to other phenomena:

> [The hermeneutical circle] is not to be reduced to the level of a vicious circle or even a circle which is merely tolerated. In the circle is hidden a positive possibility of the most primordial kind of knowing. To be sure, we genuinely take hold of this possibility only when, in our interpretation, we have understood that our . . . task is never to allow our [pre-conceptions] to be presented to us by fancy and tradition, but rather to make the scientific theme secure by examining these fore-structures in terms of the phenomena, themselves. (Heidegger, 1962, p. 148)

Heidegger further characterizes one's existence as having the characteristic of time-transcendence. *Dasein* exists not only in one's present consciousness, but also is thrown (*geworfen*) into the past, and projected into the future. Thus, existence is trans-temporal.

In his major work, *Being and Time*, Heidegger (1962) examines the construction of subjectively experienced knowledge over time. In his view, this ICR never reaches completion or finality, but rather evolves continuously within each individual as an inherently unstable and unfinished flow of existence (Heidegger, 1958). Further, knowledge and understanding of the world always follow rather than precede, the individual's existence

(Heidegger, 1968). Thus, our existence precedes our knowledge of our own identity or essence.

On this last point, the philosophy of Heidegger anticipates that of Sartre (1950, 1963). Sartre's most famous maxim—"Existence precedes essence" (1956b, p. 257)—effectively communicates the existentialist position by inverting the Cartesian Cogito: "I am; therefore, I think."

> We mean that first of all man exists, encounters himself, surges up in the world—and defines himself afterwards. If man, as the existentialist sees him, is not definable, it is because to begin with he is nothing. He will not be anything until later, and then he will be what he makes of himself. (Sartre, 1956b, p. 264)

Thus, existentialism differs (in two significant ways) from the philosophies previously considered. First, it begins by predicating only the existence of the individual, leaving open all questions concerning the external material world and thereby departing dramatically from the tenets of Material Determinism. Second, it considers all the individual's "humanness" as contributing to *Dasein* via the personal construction of knowledge and self-identity (ICR). Hence, emotions, imagination, motives, yearnings, and aspirations all participate in the creation of subjective selfhood and understanding via the Individual Construction of Reality (Sartre, 1956a).

The practical consequences of existentialist thought for consumer-behavior theory might seem to push us in the direction of relativism and subjectivism. Indeed, if each individual exists only within the process of "becoming," his or her identity and characteristics must forever remain elusive. Further, if objects and people cannot be reduced to a set of common essences or constituent attributes, each person becomes irreducibly unique and, hence, inherently noncomparable. Clearly, such a construal of "being" seriously challenges the traditional metaphysics and methods of consumer research. Yet, as MacQuarrie (1972) notes, all is not necessarily lost:

The fact that man is unfinished . . . does not mean that a description
is impossible, but that such a description must be directed to
possibilities rather than properties. The fact that each individual
is unique does not mean that we are confronted with a formless
and indescribable multiplicity, for there are limits or horizons
within which all these unique existents fall, and there are structures that can be discerned in all of them. (p. 78)

In other words, we might pursue MacQuarrie's "structures" by
searching for the common internal paths or avenues for the
development of *Dasein*.

An immediate application of existentialist philosophy to
consumer-behavior phenomena appears to lie in the areas of
esthetic, hedonic, and emotional responses (Hirschman &
Holbrook, 1982, 1986; Holbrook & Hirschman, 1982). Perhaps
more than any other form of consumption experience, such
esthetic-hedonic-emotional reactions involve the whole of consciousness: senses, thoughts, feelings, values. Further, they produce an intensity of being that often differs vividly from the
day-to-day business of life. It follows that consumers may find
it difficult to reduce such consumption experiences to verbal
labels. Thus does ICR move beyond LCR by adding an element
of profundity that reflects the human condition. To express such
aspects of the *Dasein*, consumers might often say, "I just can't
explain it to you; you had to *be there* to understand it." In such
instances of consumption, being there is what matters most.

SUGGESTED READING

Eagleton, T. (1983). *Literary theory*. Minneapolis: University of Minnesota Press.

6

RATIONALISM

Rationalism differs from Idealism in that the former adopts the epistemological position that ideas are innate and that truth emerges from the application of pure reason, whereas the latter supports the ontological view of ideas or noetic objects as the ultimate reality. Hence, epistemologically, Rationalism stands diametrically opposed to Empiricism, which holds that all ideas stem from experience, even while, ontologically, Empiricism, which encourages skepticism concerning our ability to know the existence of the material world, can cohere with Idealism (as in the work of Berkeley). For this reason, because our focus is primarily epistemological rather than ontological, we shall employ the term Rationalism to describe philosophies that place their emphasis on the role of innate ideas and/or pure reason, even where their spokespersons also happen to hold views that might be described as Idealistic.

In our view, Rationalism adopts the extreme form of Mental Determinism at one end of the philosophical continuum shown in Table 1.1. In general, it posits that all knowledge depends upon preexisting categories of mind. By relying on the innate thoughts and concepts given to pure reason, one proceeds to develop the Mental Construction of Reality or MCR. In other words, from this perspective, knowledge originates within the individual where it shapes his or her subjective experience of the external world. Thus, *homo cogitans* engages in an internal-to-external transfer of meaning by which the world is made real. One brings the world into existence by fitting it to one's previously existing mental categories and concepts. (For a good intuitive account, see Bruner, 1986.)

Modern Rationalism traces its origins back at least as far as the Greek philosophers, Plato in particular. For example, in his allegory of the cave, Plato (1968) argues for a "journey upwards" via "the ascent of the soul into the intellectual world":

> In the world of knowledge the idea of True Forms . . . is also inferred to be the universal author of all things beautiful and right, parent of light and the lord of light in this visible world, and the immediate source of reason and truth in the intellectual; and this is the power upon which he who would act rationally . . . must have his eye fixed. (p. 272)

To Plato, the external world, as viewed through the senses, was but a shadowy distortion compared with the brilliance and clarity of objects' True Forms, which existed only in the mind. Plato therefore enshrined the subjective mental image given to reason as the genesis of knowledge.

We have picked up this rationalistic impetus at the stage of the Cartesian Dualism, by virtue of which Descartes earned his reputation as the father of modern philosophy (Scruton, 1981). Descartes (1986) believed that, beginning with the self-evident cogito or "I think," he could use pure reason or "the natural light" to develop all other truths. A similar faith in the power of pure reason characterized the work of such rationalists as Spinoza, Leibniz, and Hegel. (For a review, see Scruton, 1981.) However, the epistemological implications of a thoroughgoing Rationalism are represented perhaps most clearly by the manner in which first Eberhard and then Fichte interpreted the work of Immanuel Kant:

> For Fichte, Kant's great achievement was to have shown that the mind has knowledge only through its own activity; in an important sense, the objects of knowledge are a product of that activity. (Scruton, 1982, p. 93)

Fichte's view appears to misinterpret what we earlier characterized as Kant's Interactionist perspective wherein "the principles of pure understanding can apply only to objects of the senses . . . never to things in general without regard to the mode in which we are able to apprehend them" (Scruton, 1982, p. 94). Further, this misinterpretation appears to color the somewhat confusing manner in which Bruner (1986) acknowledges his own intellectual debt to Kant. Apparently, Bruner identifies with Nelson Goodman's constructivist position that "what we call the world is a product of some mind whose symbolic procedures construct the world" (p. 95). Bruner (1986) credits Kant as the originator of this rationalistic view:

> The constructionist view, that what exists is a product of what is thought, can be traced to Kant, who first fully developed it. . . . Kant's view of the world "out there" being made up of mental products is Goodman's starting point. (p. 96)

As noted when we discussed the Interactionist aspects of Kant's thought, we do not subscribe to this Fichtean manner of reading Kant. Nevertheless, the Fichtean interpretation does highlight a rationalistic aspect of Kant's thought to which we might profitably attend.

FICHTE-KANT

Specifically, Kant (1929) did propose that the human mind contains preexisting tendencies to categorize and structure stimuli in a certain way. Thus, information "given to our senses" by the world gets transformed into a preexisting ideal form or mental category. Further, since all human observers possess the same transformative mental mechanisms, no "third party" or "objective person" exists who can adjudicate whether the forms apparent to our consciousness in any way resemble their external counterparts. From the Kantian rationalist perspective, then, the true nature of the world remains unknowable; our only knowledge comes from what our minds construct according to preexisting categories of thought.

As Seung (1982, p. 148) notes,

> The empiricist account [of knowledge] was unacceptable to rationalists for two reasons. First, it stands on a naive but implausible assumption that sense impressions of reality can be compared with reality itself. But this comparison is impossible because reality is, unlike its impressions, directly inaccessible to us. We encounter reality *only* through its *impressions*. . . . [the] originals forever escape our grasp. Second, rationalists believe in the existence of *innate ideas* whose genesis could not be explained by the empiricist account, such as the idea of causality. . . . If these ideas are innate to our subjective mind, there is no reason [to expect] them to reflect the nature of reality. (p. 148)

Indeed, Kant argued for the preordination even of the ways in which mental categories are combined and compared during decision making and logical reasoning. For example, humans have an innate tendency to project causal structures onto external events and will always tend to observe causal relationships, whether or not they actually happen to exist (a point familiar from attribution theory that Hume had forcefully anticipated). Eco (1973) makes a similar case somewhat more vividly by using a literary analogy based on the complex prose of James Joyce:

> It is only natural that life should be more like *Ulysses* than like *The Three Musketeers*; and yet we are all more inclined to think of it in terms of the Three Musketeers than Ulysses—or rather, I can

only remember and judge life if I think of it as a traditional novel. (p. 206)

That one might perceive one's life more like a realistic novel than a work of stream of consciousness fiction raises questions of clear relevance to the social sciences. Here, one illustrative position closely akin to the Fichtean-Kantian Rationalism comes from the work of Carl Jung.

JUNG

Like Fichte's interpretation of Kant, Jung proposed that meaning emanates entirely from preexisting mental structures. To Jung, humans not only arrive in the world with predispositions to categorize sensory stimuli in specific ways, but also possess innate meanings that they assign to specific sensory stimuli. Like Lévi-Strauss (discussed later), Jung reached this conclusion after extensive examination of the symbolism and mythology developed by various societies. He concluded that the striking parallels in meaning assigned to various objects by societies widely separated in time and space revealed the existence of archetypes or systematic inborn meaning structures universal to all humans of the past and present.

An example will help to clarify Jung's proposition. In many cultures, including our own, beneficent sacred powers are believed to reside in the sky (i.e., the heavens), whereas evil or destructive sacred powers are believed to dwell under the earth (i.e., hell). If the idea that heaven (hell) is a place above (below) the earth appears self-evident and natural to the reader, Jung's thesis is supported. Logically, heaven and hell could be anywhere (or nowhere). Yet we appear to share an innate predisposition to locate one above us, in the skies, and the other beneath us, in the depths of the earth.

Rationalism carries some important potential implications for consumer research. For example, the information-processing paradigm (Bettman, 1979) puts forward propositions reminiscent

of Jung or Fichte-Kant in which consumers encounter environmental information that is transformed from a jumble of sensory
data to a neat, coherent set of concepts stored in a systematic
memory structure and then brought into consciousness when
processed according to a linear, logical sequence of thought.
The existence of such mental structures and reasoning processes is deemed to be universal across all humans. To convert
the information-processing model into a rationalistic paradigm,
one need only accept the impossibility of proving a direct
correspondence between the conceptual contents of the consumer's
mind and the objective contents of the real world.

Similarly, as anticipated in our earlier discussion of essences,
the Platonic notion of true forms bears some resemblance to our
concepts of the product prototype and the ideal point. The
concept of an ideal automobile, for example, represents an
abstracted version of several, specific real cars. To turn this
model into a version of the Platonic philosophy one might
designate the idealized concept of an automobile as the true or
pure form of automobile (its "carness"), with specific "real"
cars seen as degraded or less-than-perfect copies of the ideal
car. In this view, the flow of meaning would move from the
mind to the world rather than from the world to the mind. The
mental construct thus becomes the true, perfect, or pure tem-
plate against which material objects are judged (Hirschman
1985).

SUGGESTED READING

Bruner, J. (1986). *Actual minds, possible worlds.* Cambridge, MA: Harvard Univer-
    sity Press.
Scruton, R. (1981). *From Descartes to Wittgenstein.* New York: Harper & Row.

➤ PART TWO ◄

METHODS

7

FROM PHILOSOPHY TO METHODOLOGICAL ASSUMPTIONS

In Part I of this book, we have considered a continuum of philosophies whose epistemological positions range from Material to Mental Determinism. Each possesses potential relevance to consumer-behavior theory, but cannot be fully implemented without the availability of appropriate research methods. Hence, in Part II we develop a transition from philosophy and epistemology to research methods and applications. Toward that end, we shall emphasize the pervasive role played by four key concepts: socialization, texts, vocality, and interpretation.

SOCIALIZATION

Socialization plays two important roles in discussing how diverse potential origins of knowledge may be translated into a corresponding set of research methods. First, as Berger and Luckmann (1966) note,

> The individual is not born a member of society. He is born with a predisposition toward sociality, and he becomes a member of society. . . . The beginning point of this process is internalization; the immediate apprehension or interpretation of an event as expressing meaning. . . . The ontogenetic process by which this is brought about is *socialization*, which may thus be defined as the comprehensive and consistent induction of an individual into the objective world of a society or a sector of it. (pp. 119-120)

Here, the term "objective world of a society" does not necessarily assume or exclude the existence of a tangible, material world. Rather, Berger and Luckmann (1966) state that "Every individual is born into an objective social structure within which he encounters the significant others who are in charge of his socialization" so that "their definitions of his situation are posited for him as objective reality" (p. 121). Thus, the objective world of a society into which the individual is socialized depends on that society's consensus of meaning regarding the world, facticity, and the nature of reality (Outhwaite, 1975, p. 91). This conceptualization embraces origins of knowledge that cover the complete range between the extremes of Material and Mental Determinism. Knowledge may emanate from any physical source or mind-set or from any combination of the two and still constitute the belief system of a particular society. This open perspective will provide the required versatility as we consider different research strategies for conducting inquiries across the continuum of possible knowledge origins.

Second, Berger and Luckmann (1966) also distinguish between primary and secondary socialization:

> *Primary socialization* is the first socialization an individual undergoes in childhood, through which he becomes a member of society. *Secondary socialization* is any subsequent process that inducts an already socialized individual into new sectors of his society. (p. 120)

This distinction implies both that all members of a particular society will be acculturated so as to share a common consciousness characteristic of that culture and that individuals may undergo successive further inductions into specialized bodies of knowledge and systems of belief characteristic of smaller sectors or subcultures. In each instance of primary and secondary socialization, the individual acquires the relevant consensus view of reality or SCR.

Taylor (1985, p. 39) echoes this view almost two decades later by noting:

> We can speak of a shared belief, aspiration, etc. when there is a convergence between the subjective beliefs, aspirations, of many individuals. But it is part of the meaning of a common aspiration, belief, celebration, etc. that it is not just shared but part of the common reference world. . . . Common meanings are the basis of community. Intersubjective meaning gives people a common language to talk about social reality and a common understanding of certain norms, but only with common meanings does this common reference world contain significant common actions, celebrations, and feelings. These are objects in the world that everybody shares. This is what makes community. (p. 39)

Similarly, Seung (1982) states that commonality of meaning is necessary for communication.

> It is impossible for the members of a community to interact with one another without the benefit of shared conventions, because their shared conventions constitute the context of their interactions. This sharing is what is meant by the *unity* of a culture or community, or its *objective mind*. (p. 219)

However, Berger and Luckmann (1966) also address the possibility of individual consciousness and idiosyncratic belief
systems comparable to what we earlier characterized as ICR:

> The possibility of "individualism" (that is, of individual choice
> between discrepant realities and identities) is directly linked to the
> possibility of unsuccessful socialization. We have argued that
> unsuccessful socialization opens up the question of who am I? . . . The
> individualist emerges as . . . [one] who has at least the potential to
> migrate between a number of available worlds and who has delib-
> erately and awarely constructed a self out of the "material" pro-
> vided by a number of available identities. (p. 157)

From this breadth of perspective, it follows that the Berger
and Luckmann account of the socialization process spans the
continuum of possibilities for the construction of reality—from
PCR to MCR, as depicted in Table 1.1—in effect, by espousing
the Communalism shown at the center of Figure 1.1. Note that
we argue not that all such positions are correct, but rather that
any single philosophy or combination thereof may be tenable
within a particular scientific community.

The beliefs and values constituting reality in one scientific
community will often differ from those prevailing in another
community. Thus, knowledge claims and validation procedures
accepted as appropriate in one will be inappropriate for those
practiced in another. However, within communities of inquiry,
research will be conducted and knowledge accrued according
to the rationale dictated by each group's standards. As Bernstein
(1985) notes,

> When we concentrate on the nature and role of community in
> scientific inquiry, on the ways in which rationality is essentially
> dialogic and intersubjective, then we must not only clarify the
> descriptive aspects of actual scientific communities, but their *nor-
> mative* dimensions, as well. . . . An adequate analysis must take
> account of the norms embedded in intersubjective communica-
> tion, norms which serve as regulative and critical ideals of such
> inquiry. (pp. 77-78)

TEXTS

Previously, we have cited several concepts used by philosophers to describe the knowledge systems of social groups and individuals. These have included common sense, ideology, false consciousness, alternative ideologies, *Weltanschauungen, Lebenswelt, Dasein*, collective consciousness, and archetypes. Similarly, in academic parlance, we may refer to these same conceptual notions as theories, paradigms, scientific communities, and schools of thought. The common element relating these various terms is that each refers, in one way or another, to an integrated system of beliefs about the nature of reality. Taylor (1985), for example, states that: "We ought to look at what we *do* when we theorize; when we do we see that theories serve more than descriptive and explanatory purposes, they also serve to define *ourselves*" (p. 116). In the discussion to follow, we shall unite these philosophical and academic concepts by referring to them as *texts*.

The term text in contemporary semiotic literary theory (Eco, 1979; Barthes, 1972, 1977) derives from its original reference to a distinctive narrative pattern or plot. However, its usage has now grown substantially beyond that limited context (Geertz, 1983) so that text is currently used to refer to knowledge structures as diverse as human action (Ricoeur, 1971, 1981; Eco, 1979) and movie genres (Cawelti, 1976). Thus, for example, Bloor (1983; following Melden, 1967) suggests that

> To explain an action means finding a classification in terms of wants or motives or intentions which can be sustained through an ever-widening circle of circumstances and consequences. It is like finding the reading of a text that is consistent with what follows. (pp. 72-73)

Thanks largely to the work of Ricoeur (1971, 1981), this view of action as a text has gained increasingly wide prominence in the social sciences and has helped to justify the view of social science as an act of interpretation (Hekman, 1986; Heritage, 1984).

> Ricoeur approaches this problem on the twofold assumption that meaningful action is the object of the social sciences, and that a hermeneutical discourse on such action is possible. On the basis of this assumption, Ricoeur submits that "the paradigm of reading, which is the counterpart of the paradigm of writing, provides a solution for the methodological paradox of the human sciences." (Thompson, 1981, p. 65)

Indeed, from a similar perspective, Geertz (1973) regards culture as a text and anthropology as an exercise in close reading.

> The culture of a people is an ensemble of texts, themselves ensembles, which the anthropologist strains to read over the shoulders of those to whom they properly belong. . . . As in more familiar exercises in close reading, one can start anywhere in a culture's repertoire of forms and end up anywhere else. . . . But whatever the level at which one operates, the guiding principle is the same: societies, like lives, contain their own interpretations. One has only to learn how to gain access to them. (pp. 452-453)

The utility of the term *text* for our present discussion lies in its avoidance of the undesirable connotations associated with such terms as *ideology* and *theory*, which have served to segregate the belief systems of people from those of the social scientists who observe them. As we shall argue, the texts of social scientists perform functions similar to those of other people. Notice that, although the term *text* is drawn from interpretive disciplines such as literary criticism, we do not intend to impose an interpretive value system on the reader by using this term. Rather, we intend it to apply to all five of the philosophical positions decribed earlier. For example, within an empiricist framework, text is analogous to such terms as *theory, model,* or *paradigm,* which imply a mental schema, often shared by a group of researchers, used to represent material phenomena.

In the subsequent discussion of research methods, we shall suggest that people acquire texts through socialization processes.

Thus, primary socialization leads toward submersion in the overall cultural text of a society, whereas secondary socialization encourages the acquisition of texts, or subtexts, pertinent to specific groups, segments, sectors, or subcultures. Again, individuality arises through the idiosyncratic combination, internal generation, communication, or innate possession of texts.

VOCALITY

Like text, the term *vocality* originated in linguistics and literary analysis (Levine, 1985; Griswold, 1987; Geertz, 1983). Vocality refers to the number of meanings a text may have. For example, a univocal text carries only one meaning, whereas a multivocal or plurivocal text admits two or more possible ways of construing its meaning (Ricoeur, 1976). Multivocality extends the notion of ambiguity (Empson, 1949) or polysemy in which "a single word or phrase may carry a number of meanings" (Levine, 1985, p. 20) to the recognition that entire narratives may contain or evoke multiple meanings.

Seung (1982, p. 255) provides some examples of polysemy: "In Plato's *Dialogues,* the word *pharmakon* means both remedy and poison. In Mallarme's *Mimique,* the word hymen stands for both virginity and marriage. Again in *Mimique,* the word *blanc* perpetually changes its meaning" (p. 255). More commonly, as ethnomethodologists such as Leiter (1980) have noted, words and phrases used in everyday conversation are multivocal; the listener must rely on the context in which the phrase or word appears to determine which, of many possible meanings, the speaker intended.

> Without a supplied context, objects and events have equivocal or multiple meanings. . . . The context consists of such particulars as who the speaker is, . . . his current purpose and intent, the setting in which the remarks are made, and the actual or potential relationship between speaker and hearer. (p. 107)

For example, the word *kid* may refer to a child, a young goat, or to humorous repartee; the appropriate meaning depends upon the context in which the word is used.

Thus, the potential vocality, univocal or multivocal, of a text depends on the assumptions the researcher makes about the origins of its meaning. Researchers who view texts as originating totally in the material world (i.e., complete Material Determinism) or entirely from innate mental structures (i.e., complete Mental Determinism) would perceive them as univocal. That is, the researcher would believe that there was only one relevant meaning to be discovered (Hirsch, 1967, 1976; Juhl, 1980; Lévi-Strauss 1978). Conversely, texts that researchers deem to originate from points that permit their meaning to be socially constructed and/or personally idiosyncratic may be multivocal (Ricoeur, 1976, 1981). Here, the researcher's task is discerning which, of several possible meanings, to extract from or ascribe to the text.

INTERPRETATION

As indicated earlier in our more lengthy discussion of Interpretivism, the process by which a researcher decides what meaning to associate with a given text involves interpretation (Fish, 1980). The way researchers construct interpretations of a text depends on their assumptions about its origins. If, for example, researchers assume (à la Goldmann) that the objects produced by a social group instantiate the text of that group's belief system, they will attempt to ground an analysis of that social group in the meanings associated with their cultural products.

Conversely, if they assume (à la Heidegger) that meaning resides in the existential *Dasein* of individual consciousness, they may constrain textual interpretation to the contents of their own personal thoughts and feelings (as Sartre advocates). Such interpretations, Geertz (1988) states, are "author-saturated . . . texts in which the self the text creates and the self that creates the text are represented as being very near to identical" (p. 97). Thus, the kinds of research interpretations one constructs depend inherently on the a priori assumptions one makes concerning the origins of knowledge.

Fish (1976) relates the nature of interpretation back to the scientific community that is undertaking it. When different people share the same interpretive strategies, he maintains, they constitute one *interpretive community*. To say that a text gives rise to a particular meaning suggests that this meaning will be produced by all members of the interpretive community because they share the same interpretive stance and sense of reality. Fish, a relativist, further proposes that since their interpretation assigns meaning to an amorphous, or ambiguous, text, it might as well be regarded as an act of writing rather than reading: "And if a community believes in the existence of only one text, then the single strategy its members employ will be forever writing it" (Fish, 1976, p. 478).

PREVIEW

Metaphysical assumptions and research strategies that correspond to the earlier philosophical continuum on the origin of knowledge appear in Figure 7.1 (which should be compared with Table 1.1). Toward the left side of each center panel of Figure 7.1 is the text to be interpreted. To the right of the text area are arrows indicating the directional flow of meaning between the text and the researcher. At the far right of the figure, the researcher's orientation is represented by the assumptions and strategies appropriate to the relevant philosophical position.

Conceptually, one might discuss Figure 7.1 from top to bottom, from bottom to top, or from inside to outside. The top to bottom sequence would follow the order of Chapters 2 through 6. However, to provide what we see as the clearest exposition, we shall now move from outside to inside. This means that we shall begin by discussing (A) Empiricism (the top) in Chapter 8

PHILOSOPHICAL ASSUMPTIONS

RESEARCH STRATEGIES

A. Empiricism
(Reflection of the Text)

Text ——————→ Researcher
univocal

The Text arises from the objective, external, material world and can be read directly and unambiguously by the researcher. Logical empiricism, authorial intention (Hirsch, Juhl).

B. Socioeconomic Constructionism
(Systematization of the Text)

Text ←------------→ Researcher
univocal within a culture or subculture

The Text is a social construction that can be translated univocally and unambiguously into the primary socialization experience of the researcher. Interpretation via Organization (Foucault, Geertz).

C. Interpretivism
(Translation of the Text)

Text ←——————→ Researcher
multivocal across cultures or subcultures

The Text is a social construction that reflects a worldview different from that into which the researcher has been socialized. Requires interpretive translation. "Merging of horizons" and "Verstehen hermeneutics" (Gadamer, Ricoeur).

D. Subjectivism
(Construction of the Text)

Text ←------------→ Researcher
multivocal across individuals

The Text is an external social construction upon which is imposed the personal text of the researcher. Result is a constructed, interactive interpretation. Active reading (Iser, Eagleton, Barthes).

E. Rationalism
(Creation of the Text)

Text ←—————— Researcher
univocal

Univocal, unambiguous (universal). Text imposed upon external world by the researcher. Formalism (Frye), Formal Structuralism (Lévi-Strauss).

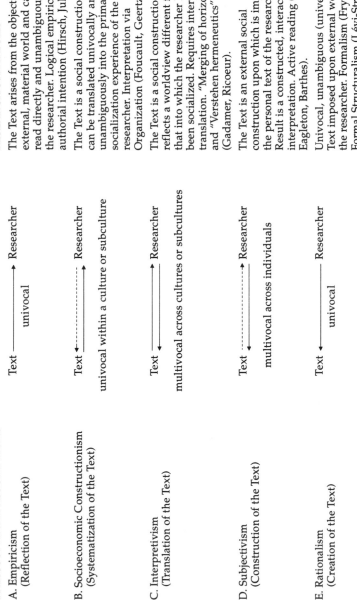

Figure 7.1. Consumer Research Strategies and Assumptions

and (E) Rationalism (the bottom) in Chapter 9 to account for the two extreme viewpoints. Then, in Chapters 10 through 12, we shall move inward to consider (B) Socioeconomic Constructionism, (C) Interpretivism, and (D) Subjectivism as alternative bases for consumer-research strategies.

SUGGESTED READING

Berger, P. L., & Luckmann, T. (1966). *The social construction of reality.* New York: Doubleday.

Fish, S. (1980). *Is there a text in this class: The authority of interpretive communities.* Cambridge, MA: Harvard University Press.

Geertz, C. (1973). *The interpretation of cultures.* New York: Basic Books.

Geertz, C. (1983). *Local knowledge: Further essays in interpretive anthropology.* New York: Basic Books.

8

EMPIRICISM
(Reflection of the Text)

Empiricism suggests that one can read a *univocal* meaning unambiguously from *direct observation of the text* itself. The a priori assumptions underlying this condition are (a) that the text is a direct product (i.e., a reification) of the material world and (b) that the researcher's consciousness is also a direct product of the same material world. Therefore, a Materially Determined text can be read unambiguously by a Materially Determined reader. In essence, this research strategy reflects commonsense empiricism, as currently embodied by logical empiricists who see consumer behavior and consumption events as physical behaviors that lend themselves to observation and measurement by objective scientific procedures (Hunt, 1983, 1984; Levine, 1985). For example, in a quote that appeared on the front page of *The New York Times*, Bobby Calder recently offered the following statement:

> Just asking people questions isn't going to reveal everything about
> them. . . . The best way to get an in-depth understanding of
> consumer values is to watch people buying and using products.
> (Foltz, 1989, p. A1; © 1989 by The New York Times Company.
> Reprinted by permission.)

Morgan and Smircich (1980) provide a more conventional
perspective on how this general strategy is translated into research practice:

> The quantitative methods used in the social sciences . . . are
> appropriate for capturing a view of the social world as a concrete
> structure. In manipulating "data" through quantitative approaches
> such as multivariate statistical analysis, social scientists are in
> effect attempting to freeze the social world into structured immo-
> bility and to reduce the role of human beings to elements subject
> to the influence of a more or less deterministic set of forces.
>   They are presuming that the social world lends itself to an
> objective form of measurement, and that the social scientist can
> reveal the nature of that world by examining lawful relations
> between elements that, for the sake of accurate definition and
> measurement, have to be extracted from their context. The large-
> scale empirical surveys and detailed laboratory experiments that
> dominate much social research stand as examples of the principal
> types of method operating on assumptions characteristic of the
> objectivist extreme of the continuum. (p. 498)

An instructive analogy to this social science strategy appears
in the theories of literary criticism advanced by Hirsch (1967,
1976) and Juhl (1980). Hirsch (1967, 1976) strongly supports the
possibility of the univocal interpretation of a text. With particular reference to the interpretation of literary texts, he recognizes possible discrepancies between the interpretation and the
actual meaning of the text due to a reader's unfamiliarity with
the genre or the author's style of language. Nevertheless, he
insists that only a single (univocal) correct interpretation exists—namely, that which conveys the author's intended meaning. Although he recognizes that readers may add or draw
additional meanings from the text, Hirsch argues that these
belong to the realm of criticism and not to the realm of valid

interpretation—i.e., to significance rather than to meaning. (Here, his proposition strongly resembles the Marxist distinction between correct ideology and false consciousness.) Thus, in his pursuit of authorial intention, Hirsch (1967) outlines an interpretive strategy closely analogous to the scientific method characteristic of logical empiricists:

> Even though we can never be certain that our interpretive guesses are correct, we know that they can be correct and that the goal of interpretation as a discipline is constantly to increase the probability that they are correct. . . . Only one interpretive problem can be answered with objectivity: "What, in all probability, did the author mean to convey?" (p. 207)

An example of this research strategy by consumer-behavior scholars appears in applications of Brunswik's (1943, 1955, 1956) Lens Model. Initiated by Huber (1975) and further developed by Holbrook (1981), Neslin (1981), and Tybout and Hauser (1981) (among others), this general approach examines the links among product features, perceptual responses, and affective evaluations via what is sometimes called the "features-perceptions-affect" or F-P-A model. The F-P-A model assumes that perceptions, the subjective impressions of sensory experience, depend upon objective product features (real properties of the material world), which they reflect with varying degrees of reliability and validity to achieve some level of "perceptual veridicality" (Holbrook & Bertges, 1981).

In keeping with the metaphysical underpinnings of their research, these investigators have relied upon a variety of statistically based inference procedures intended to calculate the accuracy of perceptual responses to the "real" or material world. In that sense, the lens is a model of perceptual or judgmental performance as gauged by the degree to which explained variance in perceptions or judgments captures the effects of stimulus features assumed to be objectively manipulable or unequivocally measurable. For example, in related research, Holbrook and Huber (1983) compared the abilities of highly trained musicians

and untrained musical novices to detect the differences between jazz saxophonists who ranged across various objectively
measurable musical features. Based on the criterion of explained variance, it turned out, somewhat surprisingly, that the
perceptual veridicalities of experts and novices were about
equal. This finding suggests that, in music at least, objective
reality makes a detectable subjective impression even in the
absence of formal training.

SUGGESTED READING

Hirsch, E. D., Jr. (1967). *Validity in interpretation.* New Haven, CT: Yale University
    Press.

9

RATIONALISM
(Creation of the Text)

At the antipodal extreme from Empiricism, Rationalism posits a knowledge flow wherein the researcher unambiguously and univocally bestows upon any external text a meaning that originates within his or her own mind. In other words, a text that preexists in the reader's mind is imposed on phenomena in the external world. Therefore, knowledge arises not from a textual source outside the researcher, but rather from a reader-to-world transference. (In this case, the investigator is perhaps more aptly termed an inscriber or writer.) Thus, Rationalism translates into a research strategy that assumes that all texts originate in the preexisting mental structures of the researcher and are subsequently projected onto the world.

The research methods based on this perspective include Formalism (Frye, 1957) and Formal Structuralism (Lévi-Strauss, 1960, 1963, 1968a & b, 1978). We shall discuss these in turn.

In his comprehensive *Anatomy of Criticism*, Northrop Frye (1957) put forward a Formalist theory of literary analysis. Frye believed that literature of all cultures and periods followed a system of objective laws.

> These laws were the various modes, archetypes, myths and genres by which all literary works were structured. At the root of all literature lay four narrative categories: comedy, romance, tragedy, and irony. . . . The modes and myths of literature [were viewed as] transhistorical. . . . Literature . . . is not to be seen as the self-expression of individual authors, who are no more than functions of this universal system: it springs from the collective subject of the human race itself, which is how it comes to embody archetypes or figures of universal significance. (Eagleton, 1983, pp. 91-93)

Frye's methodology, therefore, involves analyzing the narrative structure in a given piece of literature for the purpose of classifying it into the appropriate genre. His categorization scheme functions much like the taxonomies used by biologists and botanists to organize varieties of animal and plant life. The key difference is that, for Frye, the classifications arose from inherent mental patterns used by humans to construct literature rather than reflecting environmental processes of natural selection, as in the biological view. In this, Frye clearly espouses the Mental Construction of Reality characteristic of Rationalism. Indeed, in this light, Culler (1975) explicitly links Frye's genres with the deep structures of Chomsky's (1965) transformational grammar:

> The theory of literature of which Frye speaks can be regarded as the "grammar" or literary competence which readers have assimilated, but of which they may not be consciously aware. (Culler, 1975, p. 122)

Similarly, Lentricchia (1980) ties Frye's myths to the aforementioned rationalistic interpretation of Fichte-Kant. Myths are full-fledged Kantian structures.

> Like the forms of sensibility, time and space, or like the twelve
> categories of understanding, myths are the immovable lenses of
> vision which determine the shape of the phenomenal world. (p. 37)

An even more fully developed method of investigating as-
cribed texts grew from the structural linguistics of Saussure
(1959). As already discussed, the structuralist method applies
semiotic theory to objects and activities other than language
itself. For example, a myth, a motion picture, a shopping trip,
and a sporting event can each be viewed as a text whose coherent meaning depends on some set of laws and signifying relationships. One structural approach, which we might call Formal
Structuralism (e.g., Geertz, 1988; Lévi-Strauss, 1960, 1963, 1968a
& b, 1978) assumes that the sign system present in all human-
created texts results directly from innate, universal mental structures. Thus, in essence, Formal Structuralism holds the contro-
versial position that all cultural texts, of all people, in all historical periods, reify the same inherent mental patterns (Culler,
1975; Harrari, 1979; Seung, 1982; Wolff, 1975, 1981). Eagleton
(1983), for example, characterizes Lévi-Strauss' structural analyses of American Indian myths as follows:

> Beneath the immense heterogeneity of [these] myths were certain
> constant universal structures, to which any particular myth could
> be reduced. . . . These structures, Lévi-Strauss considered, were
> inherent in the human mind, so that in studying a body of myth
> we are looking less at its narrative content than at the universal
> mental operations which structure it. (pp. 103-104)

Lévi-Strauss (1960, 1963, 1968a, b, 1978) most commonly sought
to identify the structural relationships of binary opposition or
parallel construction, which he believed was the fundamental
pattern of all human thought and language. Thus, as Seung
(1982) notes, Structuralism proposes that "all human institutions and conventions are governed by the structural universal
of binary opposition, because they are extensions of language
and because the fundamental structure of language is binary

opposition. . . . Binary opposition is the universal structure of all languages . . . because it is the fundamental structure of the human mind" (pp. 7-8).

For example, if one actor in a myth moves upward (e.g., toward heaven), a second actor might move downward (e.g., toward hell); if one narrative character marries outside the tribe and is fertile, an opposing character might marry inside the tribe and be infertile; and so forth. Lévi-Strauss applied this notion of binary codes in an insightful fashion to all manner of texts—from food practices (Lévi-Strauss, 1968a & b) to the Wagnerian operatic Tetralogy (Lévi-Strauss, 1978). However, the method itself remains invariant. For each text, the composing acts are broken down into constituent units and then combined with other opposing units to form *mythemes* or "bundles of relations." The overall pattern formed by this fully unfolded binary code represents the structural law or deep meaning of the text.

Importantly, for consumer research, the structuralist mode of analysis is not confined to linguistic texts, but may be extended to all social phenomena having a semiological character (i.e., those with a self-sufficient system of internal relations). Thus, "the extension of this mode of analysis confers upon the social sciences a type of explanation quite different from that implied by a Humean account of causality, for structuralist explanation posits relations that are *correlative,* rather than consecutive or sequential" (Thompson, 1981, p. 65).

Here also, one might compare both Chomsky's (innate) deep structures and Freud's (unconscious) latent content (Chomsky, 1965; Freud, 1965a, 1977; Seung, 1982). With similarities to both points of view, Lévi-Strauss argues that the deep meanings generally remain unrecognized by nominal readers, because they are so innate as to be taken for granted or consciously invisible to those who attend only to the surface narrative.

This rationalistic view of Lévi-Strauss corresponds to the Fichtean interpretation of Kant and has persuaded a number of scholars that Lévi-Strauss subscribes to what we have called the Mental Construction of Reality (Hawkes, 1977, p. 88; Kurzweil,

1980, pp. 24, 231; Lentricchia, 1980, p. 127). However, Lévi-Strauss (1985) himself has rejected this rationalistic interpretation of his work as endorsing MCR and has instead allied himself with what we earlier described as Kant's Interactionism:

> The structural approach I have followed for over a quarter of a century has often been assessed by my Anglo-Saxon colleagues as "idealism" or "mentalism." I have even been labelled as Hegelian. Certain critics have accused me of seeing structures of thought as the cause of culture, sometimes even of confusing them (p. 102). . . . Rather, what we witness and try to describe are attempts to realize a sort of compromise between certain historical trends and special characteristics of the environment, on the one hand, and, on the other, mental requirements that in each area carry on previous ones of the same kind. In adjusting to each other, these two orders of reality mingle so as to make a meaningful whole. . . . There is nothing Hegelian in such a conception (p. 104). . . . Only a close collaboration between the natural and the human sciences will permit the rejection of an outmoded philosophical dualism. Instead of opposing ideal and real, . . . one will recognize that the immediate data of perception cannot be reduced to any of these terms but lies betwixt and between. (p. 118)

Sperber (1975, 1985) appears to agree with this retrospective self-assessment by Lévi-Strauss. Placing the Lévi-Straussian structuralism "in the context of the rationalist/empiricist controversy" (1985, p. 91), he supports the Anglo-Saxon view of Lévi-Strauss as assuming that "the human mind is able and liable to impose a specific kind of organization on its representation of the world" (1985, p. 75). But, he joins Lévi-Strauss in rejecting any Hegelian interpretation (1975, p. 72) and, indeed, argues that "we should depart even more from the empiricist a priori . . . and go farther in the rationalist direction in which Lévi-Strauss has made a first step" (1985, p. 75). Here, in other words, Sperber warns against repeating the kind of mistake that characterized the Fichtean interpretation of Kant, though he personally seems prepared to move in the direction of a greater rationalism than Lévi-Strauss might have intended.

As mentioned earlier, the information-processing paradigm of consumer choice (Bettman, 1979) employs many of the research assumptions advocated by Formal Structuralism—for example, the universality of thought processes and memory structures across all humans. A passage from Bettman's (1979) book clearly exemplifies this orientation:

> There is also general agreement on the structure of the storage in Long Term Memory for semantic information. Semantic storage is thought to be organized as a network of nodes and links between nodes, with the nodes representing concepts and the links denoting relationships among concepts. . . . New information is integrated by developing a configuration of links to already existing concepts. . . . The description above . . . seems to imply that a person is viewed as a computer, an IBM 360 with skin. This is not true. A person is an information processor, as is a computer, and as such both will have basic organizational similarities. However, . . . the specific components differ greatly.

An example of structural analysis applied to a consumption context is provided in Hirschman's (1988) interpretation of the television series *Dallas* and *Dynasty*. She identified "the primary structure encoded within *Dallas* and *Dynasty* [as] the binary opposition between secular consumption and sacred consumption" (p. 347).

> Secular consumption refers to the acquisition of man-made products, typically those resulting from technological processes and those sought after by consumers in a competitive fashion. Within both television series, secular consumption was associated with personality characteristics of greed, avarice, and envy. . . . Those who sought secular products as ends in themselves paid a spiritual price for them. Such characters were typically lonely, unloved, envied, and distrusted by others. . . .
> Conversely, series characters at the opposite structural pole of sacred consumption placed primary importance on virtuous objectives such as love, honor, and integrity. Sacred consumers displayed little interest in acquiring technologically produced material goods. They were not fashion conscious; they did not seek or use products in a competitive manner. . . . They were trusted by others,

TABLE 9.1

Possessions in *Dallas* and *Dynasty*

Possessions	Secular Consumption	Sacred Consumption
Dwelling	Luxurious apartment, condominium, hotel room	Handmade house, camper trailer
Transportation	Private jet, chauffeured limousine, luxury sedan, luxury sports car	Jeep, pickup truck, VW Rabbit, horse
Food	Eating in restaurants with business associates	Cooking meals at home with/for family
Apparel	Jewelry, fur coats, designer clothes (women), blue and gray business suits, tuxedos (men)	Denim jeans, leather jackets, cotton shirts, cotton dresses, work boots
Beverages	Distilled liquor, scotch, brandy, champagne	Beer, coffee
Services	Household servants, chauffeurs, waiters, detectives, lawyers, masseuses, manicurists	Services performed by the individual for self/family
Leisure	"Charity" balls, cocktail parties, Nautilus machines, swimming pools	Horseback riding, camping, picnics, playing with children, backyard barbecuing, knitting

SOURCE: Hirschman, E. C. (1988). The ideology of consumption: A structural-syntactical analysis of *Dallas* and *Dynasty*. Journal of Consumer Research. *15*, 344-359.

[and] they had a supportive network of friends and/or family members. (pp. 347-348)

To support this structural framework, Hirschman (1988) provided exemplars from the multiple semiotic codes embedded in the two series. These are depicted in the exhibit taken from Hirschman (p. 349) (see Table 9.1).

Although some aspects of the analysis used *experience-distant* concepts (Geertz, 1983)—as discussed in a subsequent section on "Interpretation As Translation"—the majority of the structure is built from presumed archetypal or universal human concepts. The primary bipolar schema of sacred/secular implicitly assumes that these categories of thought are common to all readers, as well as intended by the show's creators.

The validity of the analysis is dependent upon the reader's response to the interpretive framework. If, as Lévi-Strauss proposes, the underlying bipolar structure is universal, it should be "read" equivalently by all who viewed the same text.

SUGGESTED READING

Culler, J. (1975). *Structuralist poetics.* Ithaca, NY: Cornell University Press.
Frye, N. (1957). *Anatomy of criticism.* Princeton, NJ: Princeton University Press.

10

SOCIOECONOMIC CONSTRUCTIONISM
(Systematization of the Text)

Consumer research strategies under Condition B in Figure 7.1 assume that the world consists of a socially constructed and consensually validated common body of knowledge and that both the researcher and the text under investigation come from this same socially constructed world. Therefore, the researcher interprets the text of interest (e.g., a consumer-purchasing behavior, a movie, a series of advertisements) using knowledge structures drawn from the surrounding society and its shared reality.

This research strategy echoes the assumptions of ethnomethodology and the true consciousness of Marxism. As Leiter (1980) notes, "Ethnomethodologists have their reasons for studying commonsense knowledge."

The main rationale is the fact that social reality is constituted through [this] meaning and people's meaning-endowing activities. Social reality as social interaction is carried out through the use of commonsense rationalities and the stock of knowledge at hand. . . . The study of commonsense knowledge is a way of studying macro phenomena where they really count—the level of everyday life. (p. 20)

Thus, "the sociologist, like other members of society, uses the [common] sense of social structure as a resource" (p. 82).

Similarly, Geertz (1983) discusses the importance of the researcher's possession of "the informal annotation of everyday experience we call *common sense*" (p. 69). This is because "in order to follow a baseball game one must [a priori] understand what a bat, a hit, an inning, a left fielder, a squeeze play, a hanging curve, and a tightened infield are" (p. 69).

The incremental knowledge added by such investigations systematically organizes and classifies the content of social texts using terminology already present within the surrounding culture. Under these conditions, social science aims at generating a deeper understanding of cultural phenomena using language whose meaning is accessible to the general population. The societal analyses formulated by Veblen (1967), as well as sociological treatises such as those by Baltzell (1964), Foucault (1965, 1970, 1973, 1977), and C. Wright Mills (1956), represent this research strategy. In consumer-behavior research, illustrative articles by Levy (1981), Holbrook and Grayson (1986), and Belk, Sherry, and Wallendorf (1988) follow this same pattern.

Levy (1981), for example, provides an effective use of commonsense knowledge to interpret the meaning of food in American society:

Along with age and sex dimensions . . . , social class distinctions are pervasive. These are interwoven; thus there is a tendency to equate higher social position with strength, maturity, and food professionalism, and lower status preferences with softness, greasiness, and sweetness. Going up the [social status] scale, ease of preparation yields increasingly to elaboration of methods, greater use of herbs and spices, and usage of unusual foods and ingredients. (p. 56)

Clearly, the concept of social class already exists in our society, but Levy's analysis shows how specific consumption beliefs are socially linked to this more abstract concept. Thus, he takes knowledge and meaning structures already consensually accepted and organizes them into a systematic framework. The researcher does not generate a novel theory so much as he provides us with the opportunity to recognize a preexisting pattern of social meaning.

In a related way, Holbrook and Grayson's (1986) semiotic analysis of the movie *Out of Africa* demonstrated the application of shared conventions to a socially constructed text. However, it represented an extension of Levy's approach through its explicit use of part-whole hermeneutics (Geertz, 1983) to oscillate between the specifics of textual details and the overarching meaning or *Gestalt* of the text as a whole. To construct an interpretation in this way, the researcher must repeatedly "tack" (Geertz, 1983) between the social particulars and the societal framework of the text.

Geertz (1983) describes this research strategy as

a continuous dialectical tacking between the most local of local detail and the most global of global structure in such a way as to bring them into simultaneous view. . . . Hopping back and forth between the whole conceived through the parts that actualize it and the parts conceived through the whole that motivates them, we seek to turn them . . . into explications of one another. (p. 69)

Writing even more recently, Geertz (1988) has also noted the role of a common knowledge or a common sense of social reality shared between the researcher and his or her audience in this form of inquiry.

This strategy rests most fundamentally on the existence of a very strictly drawn and very carefully observed narrative contract between writer and reader. The presumptions that *connect* the author and his audience, presumptions that are social, cultural, and literary at once, are so strong and pervasive, so deeply institutionalized, that very small signals can carry very big messages. (p. 58)

Geertz's applied anthropological method essentially reiterates the earlier, hermeneutic tradition founded by Wilhelm Dilthey. Dilthey defined the *objective mind* of a community as the objectification of the patterns of thinking and feeling shared by the members of that community; as such, the objective mind expresses the common sense of the community (Seung, 1982, p. 217). In the context of consumer research, the corresponding analytic approach is illustrated by the following passages from Holbrook and Grayson (1986) in which the authors construct propositions pertaining to permanence versus loss depicted in the text of the motion picture *Out of Africa*:

> Karen Blixen's house and its contents encapsulate her stubborn devotion to European civility and are her bastion of strength and security. . . . But again, entropy reigns. Eventually, with the destruction of her crops, everything the Baroness owns must be sold. Near the movie's end, we find Karen, bereft and forlorn, wandering among a few unwanted pieces of furniture left over from her rummage sale. This scene signals her material and spiritual devastation.
>
> The constant oscillation in *Out of Africa* between conventional felicities and feral realities, between civilized pleasantries and nature red in tooth and claw, underscores the film's most central theme—namely, that all things fall apart, that everything runs down, that nothing endures, that no possession lasts forever. . . . Eventually one loses everything—one's oxen and cattle (which can be eaten by lions), one's chattel (which can be repossessed by the bank), and one's paramours (who remain free to leave at any time). (p. 377)

Notice that this analysis in no way attempts to tap into the African sensibility. Rather, it focuses on Western themes and aspects of consumption symbolism familiar to members of the general European and American community. Thus, when it is assumed that researcher, text, and research audience are "of the same social fabric," the research strategies of common sense interpretation and objective-mind hermeneutics become effective methods.

In perhaps the most ambitious example of this type of general approach reported thus far, Belk, Sherry, and Wallendorf (1988) describe the results of a pilot study that preceded the Consumer-Behavior Odyssey. This study used the methods of naturalistic inquiry (Lincoln & Guba, 1985) or humanistic inquiry (Hirschman, 1986) to explore four themes that emerged from their contacts with informants at a swap meet: freedom versus rules, boundaries versus transitions, competition versus cooperation, and sacred versus profane. For example, the report describes the sales transaction as the transforming of sacred resources into profane or secular resources:

> Sacred items are those imbued with special meaning and therefore set apart from the everyday, ordinary world of profane commodities. The transformation from the sacred to the profane is exemplified by the one-time sellers' conversion of their used personal goods into marketable wares. That is, we can interpret their primary activity as that of transforming sacred personal possessions into profane commercial wares. (p. 465)

The Odyssey piece exemplifies well the assumptions of validity made within the SCR research strategy. Belk, Sherry, and Wallendorf employed several procedures designed to insure that their interpretation was grounded in a commonly experienced, socially constructed reality. Among these were researcher *memoing*, the maintenance and comparing of *journals* among researchers, *member checks* conducted with persons in the subject population, and the use of *external auditors* (see Miles & Huberman, 1984 for a discussion of these procedures). For example, the authors describe the use of member checks as follows: "A member check involves providing all or a portion of a final report to people who have served as informants on the project. . . . Their commentary on the interpretations in the report is sought as a check on the viability of interpretations"

(p. 455). Similarly, external auditors play a role in providing a validity reference for the interpretation against a commonly held view of reality:

> Three peers familiar with the conduct and interpretation of naturalistic research were provided with complete data sets and were asked to examine the report for its grounding in the data. . . . Their task as auditors was to criticize the project for lack of sufficient data . . . if they saw such a void. . . . Also, auditors were asked to comment on the extent to which they saw the findings *flowing from* the data rather than *being imposed by* the biases of the inquirers. (p. 456)

These excerpts reveal the researchers' implicit desire to ground their interpretation in a communally shared view of the data they had collected via observations in the field. Note that they see the interpretation as desirably flowing from the external data text toward the researchers. The use of member checks and auditing procedures is designed to create a *rational consensus* regarding the meaning of the phenomena under investigation. Such a view may be likened to that of Habermas, who "maintains that truth is a validity claim which is connected with constative speech-acts" so that "a statement is true when . . . [it] would command the consent of anyone else who could enter into a discussion with the speaker" (Thompson, 1981, p. 99). That is, "the assertion of a statement is justified if and only if that statement would command a rational consensus among all who could enter into a discussion with the speaker" (Thompson, 1981, p. 198).

Analogously, Seung (1982) argues that the domain of socially constructed reality (SCR) can serve as a viable standard for establishing the validity of a given inquiry: "Whatever can be agreed upon by members of a community can be accepted as objective or true, at least within that community" (p. 230). Therefore, in the Odyssey study, the relevant community within which Belk and colleagues validate their interpretation includes the members of the population they studied and their researcher peers.

SUGGESTED READING

Lincoln, Y. S., & Guba, E. G. (1985). *Naturalistic inquiry.* Beverly Hills, CA: Sage.
Miles, M. B., & Huberman, A. M. (1984). *Qualitative data analysis.* Newbury Park, CA: Sage.

11

INTERPRETIVISM
(Translation of the Text)

U nder the assumptions of Interpretivism in Condition C of
Figure 7.1, the text under investigation is again assumed to
be a product of collective social consensus (for example, to
represent the meaning structure of a culture, subculture, or particular historical period). However, unlike Condition B (as described earlier in Chapter 10), Interpretivism also assumes that the
researcher comes from a different primary culture or at least a
different secondary subculture (Berger & Luckmann, 1966).

To accomplish this interpretive research strategy the investigator must act as a *translator*, translating concepts encountered
in one context into those appropriate to another context. Geertz
(1983) refers to these two sets of concepts as *experience-near* and
experience-distant:

> An experience-near concept is . . . one that someone might himself
> naturally and effortlessly use to define what he or his fellows see,

feel, think, imagine, and so on, and which he would readily understand when similarly applied by others. An experience-distant
concept is one that specialists of one sort or another . . . employ to
forward their scientific, philosophical, or practical aims. "Love" is
an experience-near concept; "object cathexis" is an experience-
distant one. (p. 57)

The need to translate from experience-near to experience-
distant contexts may arise in at least three different situations
within consumer research (and, indeed, within any social science). We shall discuss each in turn.

FROM THE COMMON CULTURE OF CONSUMPTION
TO A SCIENTIFIC SUBCULTURE

First and perhaps most commonly, in consumer behavior, a
researcher may attempt to interpret an assumed common culture event—an aspect of consumption or a product—using a
subcultural social science text. An example of such an interpretation appears in Hirschman's (1987a) application of the Jung-
ian concepts of *anima* and *animus* to interpret the meaning of
the motion picture *Tootsie:*

> The motion picture *Tootsie* extends the archetype of the hero along
> an orthogonal dimension. In Jungian psychology two complemen-
> tary archetypes are the anima and animus. In each individual,
> posits Jung, there is both the potential for a feminine nature (the
> anima) and a masculine nature (the animus). We are not complete
> human beings, Jung posits, unless both our anima and animus are
> fully developed and integrated. There are two ways of accomp-
> lishing this. The traditional way has been for women to develop
> only their anima and for men to develop only their animus. Unity
> and integration are achieved when the fully-feminine woman and
> the fully-masculine man unite to form a 'completed' couple. How-
> ever, an alternative way to completion is for an individual man or
> woman to develop both the anima and animus internally; such
> people would be termed androgynous in current sex role termi-
> nology and would appropriately mate (unite) with other "complete"

individuals. The plot of *Tootsie* concerns itself with exactly these issues. (p. 341)

These concepts were applied to the storyline. Here, a brief excerpt may serve to illustrate the tone of the resulting interpretation:

> Once he has been cast in the role of Dorothy, Michael begins to see life as if he were a woman. In short, his *anima*, long dormant, begins to develop. . . . [Conversely, Julie] is in the process of developing her *animus*. . . . Thus, we are presented with a man developing his *anima* and a woman developing her *animus*, who are being drawn emotionally to one another. (pp. 345-346)

In this example, the experience-distant concepts of *anima* and *animus* are used to describe and categorize experience-near events portrayed in the motion picture narrative. Analogously, a recent piece by Belk, Wallendorf, and Sherry (1989) utilizes an iterative "tacking" (Geertz, 1983) procedure that moves between social science theories on religion and common consumption phenomena, which the authors encountered during the Consumer-Behavior Odyssey of 1986. The researchers apply several technical or specialized (experience-distant) concepts— e.g., hierophany, kratophony, opposition to the profane, contamination, sacrifice, objectification, ritual, and communitas—to phenomena they encountered which, they believe, exemplify these concepts in everyday (experience-near) consumption.

For example, in discussing the consumption process of collecting, they write that "Collectors often *sacralize* objects by finding and rescuing them from those who do not understand the object's worth or value."

> For example, a collector of Mickey Mouse items found some original Disney display backdrops at a swap meet, where they were being used as tarps to cover and protect other merchandise that was considered valuable. He was proud to have rescued them and was now using them "appropriately" as backdrops to the Disney items he sells. He priced the backdrops at $500, because he did not want to sell them. (p. 20)

Thus, in this passage, these researchers attempt to *translate* an experience-near text of common consumption phenomena (Mickey Mouse) into the experience-distant text used by a secondary subculture of social scientists (sacralization).

FROM ONE SCIENTIFIC SUBCULTURE TO ANOTHER

Second, in the investigation of subcultures within one's own culture, the subculture investigated may differ from that in which the researcher was socialized. Anderson (1986) provides a somewhat unusual but instructive example of this in his enlightening description of the attempts by consumer researchers to connect their own disciplinary meaning with the expectancy-value model of attitude developed (within the context of social psychology) by Fishbein and others. Anderson subtly but revealingly describes the controversy that surrounded various attempts to translate the social psychological text of attitude theory into a consumer-oriented text concerning consumption behavior. Here, he notes that opposing combatants in the debate often owed their primary intellectual allegiance (i.e., secondary socialization) either to social psychology or to consumer behavior and, thus, that they represented worldviews tied to different a priori meaning structures (i.e., based on different socially constructed texts).

FROM CULTURE TO CULTURE

Third, and perhaps most obviously, comparable conditions may hold in cross-cultural consumer research. Here, researchers who have received primary and secondary socialization in a particular worldview (e.g., American consumer-behavior theory) attempt to apply that a priori text—for example, that of the diffusion paradigm (Robertson & Gatignon, 1986)—to interpreting consumer behavior in a foreign culture (e.g., the adoption of some innovation in a Third World Country). An example is provided by Arnould (1989):

> Four ethnographic cases from Zinder, Niger facilitate evaluation of Gatignon and Robertson's proposition. . . . The ethnographic cases target several areas of theory and method building identified by Robertson and Gatignon. One area is in understanding the effects of specific consumption decisions on consumption system objectives and vice versa. A second focuses upon indirect (economic, cultural, and historical) antecedents and effects on innovations and their diffusion. A third examines the question of perceived innovation characteristics. (p. 240)

In this example, Arnould (1989), an American-trained anthropologist, applies an American social science theory (a priori text) to consumption phenomena in a country having a different social structure and a different economic system from those of the American setting where he was trained and where the theory was developed. In such cases, interpretive strategies that integrate the disparate texts of the observer's and informant's culture are required. These are discussed further in following material.

THE GENERAL INTERPRETIVE STRATEGY

Although we have presented examples of three contexts in which the conditions assumed by Interpretivism may hold (Panel C in Figure 7.1), we have not yet explicated the method itself. Perhaps the best model of this approach for researchers in the social sciences appears in the work of Gadamer (1974-1975, 1975, 1976). Gadamer's view of the hermeneutic process differs from Dilthey's approach in that, as described earlier, it includes a self-corrective feedback loop centered around the ideal of *Verstehen* (understanding) and is intended to adjust for the fact that the researcher and the object of inquiry may not come from the same socially constructed world. In this case, the interpreter is in some sense "alienated" or "exiled" from the text. The aim, therefore, is to achieve a rapprochement between two different worldviews in a way that recognizes the unique qualities of each but establishes a common basis for communication.

Gadamer (1975), metaphorically conceives this interpretive achievement as the fusion of two disparate horizons—that of the text and that of the researcher.

> Every encounter with tradition that takes place within historical consciousness involves the experience of the tension between the text and the present. The hermeneutic task consists in not covering up this tension by attempting a naive assimilation, but [in] consciously bringing it out. This is why it is part of the hermeneutical approach to project a historical horizon that is different from its own. (p. 273)

Thus, the hermeneutical task, as Gadamer sees it, is to attain a fusion of the horizon of the text with that of the researcher. Such a fusion engenders meaning. Or, as Geertz (1988) describes the process, "it is how to get an I-witnessing author into a they-picturing story" (p. 84).

In Gadamer's view, researchers can never "escape" their pre-judgments or preexisting mental structures in attempting to interpret culturally distant texts. But, for Gadamer, such forestructures of meaning aid the researcher in constructing an understanding of the text. Indeed, they are essential to comprehension; for without some preexisting mental concepts, no meaning is possible (Bernstein, 1985, p. 137). According to Gadamer (1976), this enabling role of preconceptions is consistent with the fact that

> every finite present has its limitations. We define the concept of "situation" by saying that it represents a standpoint that limits the possibilities of vision. Hence, an essential part of the concept of situation is the concept of "horizon." The horizon is the range of vision that includes everything that can be seen from a particular vantage point. (p. 271)

For Gadamer (1976), "the horizon is something that moves with us" so that "horizons change for a person who is moving" and "this motion becomes aware of itself" (p. 271).

[Prejudices] are simply conditions whereby we experience something—whereby what we encounter *says something to us.* This
formulation certainly does not mean that we are enclosed within
a wall of prejudices and only let through the narrow portals those
things that can produce a pass saying "Nothing new will be said
here." Instead we welcome that guest who promises something
new to our curiosity. (p. 9)

Thus, as a fundamental proposition, Gadamer's hermeneutics assumes that understanding always depends on the viewpoint of the person who understands. One's own beliefs and
worldview invariably and inevitably enter the hermeneutic act and
contribute to the interpretation. Following Heidegger, Gadamer
(1975) accepts the utility of preconceptions or prejudices, which
he terms "conditions of understanding" (p. 245), on the grounds
that if we had no a priori meaning structures to guide our initial
approach to a text, we could not begin to interpret it at all
(Wolff, 1981). Hence, Gadamer's concept of the Hermeneutic
Circle envisions the process of interpretation as both interactive
and iterative. Interactively, the researcher first approaches a
text with preconceived ideas that are necessarily projected onto
the object of interpretation. However, iteratively, through contact with the meaning structure of the text, projection back onto
the researcher alters the initial preconceptions and establishes
a basis for commonality upon which to construct subsequent
refinements of understanding.

Further, as Sperber (1987) observes, such hermeneutic inquiry may cause us to reexamine our own current beliefs and
ideas and to alter them in light of the text we are interpreting.

If reading Malinowski's *Argonauts,* Bateson's *Naven,* or Evans-
Pritchard's *Nuer Religion* contributes to our understanding of ourselves and the world in which we live . . . it is because they give
us an insight into some fragments of human experience, and this,
by itself, makes it worth the journey. (p. 34)

Ricoeur (1965, 1973) states similar views on this iterative and
interactive process of rapprochement.

The purpose of all interpretation is to conquer a remoteness, a distance between the cultural epoch to which the text belongs and the
interpreter himself. By overcoming this distance . . . the exegete can
appropriate its meaning to himself: foreign, he makes it familiar, that
is, he makes it his own. It is thus the growth of his own understanding
that he pursues through his understanding of the other. (p. 101)

In sum, viewed more broadly, the hermeneutics of Gadamer
involves a negotiated or dialectical *Verstehen* in which we re-
align ourselves with the meaning structures of another culture
or subculture and modify our own view of the world, our own
construction of reality, and our own horizon of understanding,
accordingly. Such self-directed resocialization can not (and need
not) ever reach completion, but it can at least provide a pathway
for interpretive insight. Or, as Bernstein (1985) argues:

It is precisely in and through an understanding of alien cultures
that we can come to a more sensitive and critical understanding
of our own culture and of those prejudices that may lie hidden
within us. (p. 36)

In the previously mentioned research by Arnould (1989), an
American a priori text (Gatignon and Robertson's model of
innovation diffusion) is examined against the cultural text of
new product adoption in Niger. Using an iterative interpretive
strategy, Arnould prescribes revisions in the American text to
render it more congruent with the Nigerien experience:

The diffusion process in Zinder, Niger resembles a low cognition,
low involvement model at the individual level, so Gatignon and
Robertson's Proposition 18 needs revision. . . . Instead of the schema
of awareness, knowledge, attitude formation, trial, and adoption
alleged to describe Western consumer decision making, diffusion
in Zinder typically begins with group awareness and familiarity,
often followed by surrogate evaluation and trial, and then group
adoption. (p. 255)

It is possible that, as Bernstein notes, this revised version of
the diffusion model for Niger may, in turn, cause American

consumer researchers to reexamine this phenomenon in their own culture.

SUGGESTED READING

Geertz, C. (1988). *Works and lives: The anthropologist as author*. Stanford, CA: Stanford University Press.

12

SUBJECTIVISM
(Construction of the Text)

The assumptions underlying Subjectivism, as represented by Condition D in Figure 7.1, push the logics developed in Conditions B and C to their ultimate conclusion. That is, the case in which meaning is conferred upon a socially constructed external text via a deepened probing of the idiosyncratic, introspective, impressionistic world of the researcher. Thus, this research context corresponds to the assumptions underlying the phenomenological and existential philosophies of Husserl and Sartre. We might refer to the construction of an interpretation under these conditions as an *active* reading.

The assumptions underlying Subjectivism in Condition D acknowledge that any external text will suggest multivocal meanings to individual researchers. It will engender a different interpretive response in every researcher due to the unique perspective that each researcher will bring to the interpretive task (Seung, 1982, p. 194). Thus, as noted by Bernstein (1985), under this research strategy "it makes no sense to speak of *the* single or *the* correct interpretation. We recognize that there can be a variety of interpretations" (p. 125). Such interpretations are

> doubly infinite because of the limitless variety of each individual sphere of experience and because of the innumerable plurality of individual perspectives of the world. (Ricoeur, 1973, p. 125)

Within this "plurality of individual perspectives," one can discern three contrasting methodological strategies, one leaning towards phenomenology, another towards existentialism, and another towards psychoanalysis. We shall discuss each briefly.

PHENOMENOLOGICAL STRATEGIES

First, the phenomenological strategy characterizes the work of Eagleton (1983) and Iser (1978). Eagleton (1983) describes this interpretive method as follows:

> The reader will bring to the work [text] certain "pre-understandings," a dim context of beliefs and expectations within which the work's various features will be assessed. As the reading process proceeds, however, these expectations will themselves be modified by what we learn from the text, and the hermeneutical circle . . . will begin to revolve. Striving to construct a coherent sense from the text, the reader will select and organize its elements into consistent wholes. . . . He or she will try to hold different perspectives within the work simultaneously, or shift from perspective to perspective in order to build up an integrated [interpretation]. . . . As we read, we shed assumptions, revise beliefs, make more and more complex inferences and anticipations; each sentence opens up a horizon which is confirmed, challenged or undermined by the next. (p. 77)

Iser (1978) takes a similar phenomenological approach to the construction of an interpretation, referring to the process as a "dynamic interaction between text and reader" (p. 107).

The fulfillment [of the interpretation], however, takes place not in the text, but in the reader, who must activate the interplay of [mental] correlates prestructured by the sequence of sentences. . . . The sentences set in motion a process which will lead to the formation of the aesthetic object as a correlative [meaning structure] in the mind of the reader. [The resulting interpretation] is a product of the interaction between text and reader, and so cannot be exclusively traced back to the external text or the disposition of the reader. (p. 119)

Up to a point, these passages from Eagleton and Iser recall Gadamer's preoccupation with the fusion of horizons. Notice, however, how Iser concludes his description of method by reiterating the phenomenological notion of meaning coconstituted between the self and the world:

Thus the meaning of the text can only be fulfilled in the reading subject and does not exist independently of him; just as important, though, is that the reader, in constituting the meaning, is also constituted. (p. 150)

The validation of phenomenological interpretation, analogously, must lie in the response of the researcher to the phenomena of interest: "Its ultimate objective is the examination and justification of all our beliefs, both ordinary and scientific, by the test of intuitive perception" (Wolff, 1975, p. 13). Thus, phenomenological researchers must validate their interpretations against personal beliefs and values. They must seek out self-truth and self-meaning as the ultimate test for the "rightness" of an interpretation.

Recent work by consumer researchers has argued for phenomenological accounts of the consumption experience. For example, in a Special Topic Session at the Association for Consumer Research organized by Fennell (1985), that author and her colleagues developed the case for phenomenological approaches to consumer research. A more recent paper by Thompson, Locander, and Pollio (1989) provides an excellent overview.

Clearly, this phenomenological thrust is sympathetic to the present authors' focus on the experiential aspects of consumption (Holbrook & Hirschman, 1982). Thus far, few phenomenological accounts have found their way into the literature on consumer behavior. To compensate partially for this neglect, we present two examples. The first is a first-person narrative written by the second author as a description of his experiences with airline travel; the second is excerpted from an excellent treatise by Thompson, Locander, and Pollio (1990).

Morris Fears Flying

Ever since earthlings first made tentative progress toward their longing to fly, aviation has promised a consumption experience divorced from terrestriality in ways that suspend conventional norms and place passengers in a world governed by its own internal rules and ineluctable logic. Whatever their intentions, the adventures of the Wright Brothers at Kittyhawk began an aspect of a consumption Lebenswelt set apart from ordinary reality; a world in which normal expectations are suspended and replaced by a consumption system that makes sense only unto itself in a realm of aerologic and planespeak.

I climb aboard one of the few taxis whose driver seems interested in stopping for someone obviously bound for the airport (where his turnaround time is likely to be measured in hours rather than minutes). "LaGuardia, Delta," I say telegraphically. "Delta gets you there," he replies, cheerfully showing off his command of the familiar advertising theme. After a grueling tour of the teeming Manhattan streets and crowded Triboro Bridge, I arrive at the Delta terminal, standing forlornly by itself in a deserted corner of the LaGuardia Airport.

On an airline, the conventional rules of civility and sociability are suspended and replaced by planespeak and aerologic. From the moment they enter the airport, people are treated like aliens, enemies, and animals—or sometimes all three simultaneously. At the check-in counter, I encounter the first in a series of lines. It will be followed in all-too-rapid succession by the line getting onto the plane, the line of aircraft at the takeoff runway, the line getting off the plane, the line at the baggage claim area, and the ultimate exasperation of the line at the taxi stand—a veritable line of lines or a sort of metaline that knows no end. Air travel involves a level of enforced patience that makes Type-A personalities sorry they came.

The result of my first queuing experience is a personal transfiguration from the qualitative status of human to the quantitative rank of numerical digit: Flight 483, Gate 6, Seat 39A. As I proceed toward the gate, I pass through a transitional state as suspected alien intruder. My briefcase, hand luggage, shoulder bag, and overcoat must pass through an X-ray machine. My body must pass through metal detectors miraculously sensitive to the most minute amounts of pocket change or the smallest number of house keys, but apparently not able to detect arsenal-sized collections of handguns and grenades. Amazingly, as I am detained, or relieved of the contents of my pockets, and perhaps even frisked or strip-searched, I experience something approaching gratitude. Perhaps one instinctively interprets these security precautions as a sign of safety: "If they treat *me* like this, then surely they would catch a vicious terrorist before he or she got onto the plane." Naturally, we know that often they do not.

After negotiating the humiliating experience of the security check, I pass to the next phase of phenomenological airline reality: the wait at the gate. For some reason yet to receive careful scientific investigation, all planes commence the cumbersome boarding procedure at a time too late for the aircraft to have any chance at all of departing on schedule. The annoying things are that (1) this is an infallible and unbroken rule, (2) everyone has tacit knowledge of this phenomenon, and (3) nobody seems to care. A flight scheduled to depart at 2:59 p.m., if it is unusually punctual, will board at 3:01 p.m. The boarding procedure, which involves an amazing tangle of bodies, luggage, and outerwear, consumes a minimum of 35 minutes so that the plane invariably leaves the gate at least 37 minutes late. Perhaps the airlines rationalize that most planes tend to make up time on the flight (raising the interesting metaphysical issue of how the wind can *always* be blowing in the right direction). Apparently, it is necessary to start late in order to avoid any possibility of causing passengers to face the potentially terrifying implications of arriving early.

At any rate, the boarding ritual constitutes a near orgy of rule violations on the part of world-weary travelers goaded by their totalitarian aeronautical tormentors. Directives emanating from people wearing blue police-like uniforms command those seated in rows 30 and higher to begin boarding the plane. Ignoring this request, passengers in all rows immediately converge on the entrance ramp, clutching huge hanging clothes carriers, massive

satchel-like purses, overflowing shopping bags from Blooming-
dale's and Zabar's, and nearly trunk-sized pieces of hand luggage.
Loudspeakers blare the warning that all carryons must be small
enough to fit under the seat in front of you or must be stored
securely in the overhead racks. Somehow, few do and few are.
Then there commences a panicked period of desperation in which
frantic travelers attempt to cram most of their portable worldly
possessions into tiny elevated compartments just slightly out of
reach and looking smaller than the proverbial breadbox.

Eventually, this surrealistic scene subsides, and all passengers
are dutifully strapped to their seats while the giant plane lethar-
gically taxies toward one more vast, communal queue near the
takeoff strip. Lest the now-imprisoned travelers suffer from any
moments of tedium, the stewards and stewardesses now mount a
carefully choreographed audio-visual presentation (complete with
verbal commentary broadcast over a crackling PA system, visual
cues provided by vacant-looking mannequins with frozen smiles,
and supplementary printed instructional material thoughtfully
placed in the back of the seat in front of you). They cheerfully
inform their charges about the proper procedures in the event that
the air supply is cut off and the travelers need to breathe through
a tube or the plane drops into the sea and they need to escape
through one of the window exits conveniently located toward the
front and rear of the plane (far away from where I am sitting, I
note, ruefully). The good news is that the seat to which I am
strapped will float. Also, a life vest may or may not be stored
underneath. (I am never quite sure. Apparently, neither are they.)

At this point, the very moment when I feel most vulnerable and
most captive, the peculiar force of aerologic takes over almost
completely. No sooner have the plane's wheels left the ground
than bells begin to ring, signalling that one is now permitted, and,
implicitly, encouraged to smoke. (Why it is dangerous for people
to smoke during takeoff—when, presumably, they need it most—
is one of life's little mysteries for which one can only be grateful.)
At any rate, now that the passengers have been encouraged to light
up by the nearly Pavlovian force of the ringing bells, they begin
puffing huge clouds of noxious fumes in the general direction of
the nonsmoking section (for whose privileged access I have vigor-
ously lobbied with the cruelly indifferent reservations clerk). In a
matter of minutes, I find myself breathing in the choking clouds
of poisonous vapors that emanate from the rear of the plane.

At this propitious moment, even if it is only 4:00 in the after-
noon, dinner arrives. It is almost always something indescribably

dreadful and partly contained in physically unopenable packages. Dinner is followed about a half-hour later by what purports to be the cocktail hour. Would I now like, perhaps, a martini to wash down my cold lasagna or a warm beer to complement my stale brownie?

Apparently, the man sitting next to me subscribes to the airline's assessment of appropriate alimentation. He orders a gin-and-ginger-ale and then adds that he wants two gins (for a total investment of $5). When asked if he also needs two ginger ales, he replies that he does not, gulps down most of the carbonated goo, and pours the two little bottles of Tanqueray (what a waste) into what's left of the soda pop. Apparently, the resulting mixture lacks sufficient sweetness for his taste (such as it is) because he now pulls out a stick of sugarless gum (wouldn't want any cavities) on which to munch while he sips his gin fizz. Any plans I had entertained for eating vanish into the fetid air around me.

By this time it is nearly 5 p.m. I have finished dinner and cocktails (in that order), and the crew is now ready to stage its final assault on my sensibilities from the vantage point of aerologic. Suddenly, in a dramatic coup de raison, the entire plane is plunged into darkness. No explanation ever appears for why I must sit in the dark for three hours between 5 and 8 p.m. But sit in the dark I must. If I am lucky, the overhead light points vaguely in my direction and I can glance at a few magazine photos under this thin and errant illumination. Or I can shop for aeromerchandise by thumbing through the gift catalogue that clutters up the pouch on the back of the seat in front of me. Do I need an electrical converter/adaptor set that plugs into all foreign outlets for only $38.50, a money converter/passport case that instantly translates any foreign currency into any other for only $26.95, or a personalized gear shift knob with my initials engraved in brass for only $15.95? Or I can plan my next family excursion while perusing the brochure for dream vacations also located in my seatback pouch. Hawaii, Nassau, France/England (apparently a new hybrid country that one can visit only in something called a "Eurocar"), and even Freeport (otherwise feared by knowledgeable tourists as the scourge of the Bahamas) sound delightful compared to where I am right now. *Anywhere* sounds delightful compared to where I am right now.

At this point, I either do or do not have to go to the bathroom. The general rule is that if I am sitting next to the window and must climb over two sleeping bodies to get to the aisle, I do. If not, I don't. But the person who is sitting next to the window does. Either way, I lose. My next fifty minutes are spent hopping up and down while everybody in the row, except the person on the aisle, jockeys for position in the line for the water closet which is always located, with murderous intent, in the midst of the smoking section.

Finally, more bells and flashing lights signal the end of the period during which smokers are allowed to pollute the aircraft at will. Announcements begin in preparation for landing. In fluent planespeak, I am asked to put away my fold-down tray (thereby raising the issue of what to do with the half-full cup of coffee that the stewardess forgot to collect) and am invited to entertain the dubious premise that, according to aerologic, the plane cannot land as long as my seat is in the reclining position (though the rationale for this austere demand escapes detection).

Steadied by the absence of smoking and reclining, if I am very lucky, the plane now gracefully glides onto the runway—amidst bated breath but, I hope, no need for an external oxygen supply. Suddenly, another miraculous transformation occurs. Hundreds of nearly catatonic bodies spring to life and fill the aisles, while shrieking amplified voices proclaim the dire consequences that will occur if people do not remain comfortably seated until the airplane has reached a complete stop at the passenger terminal.

When that happy moment finally arrives, I brace myself for a little more good-natured pushing and shoving, while the other passengers all try to make sure that they arrive at the baggage claim area minutes or even hours before their luggage. After another inexplicable ritual in which armed guards vigilantly inspect claim checks for all suitcases carrying green tickets, but do not so much as cast an indifferent glance at any bags from which the green tickets have been removed, I push toward the comparative freedom of the outdoor wait for a taxi. I am also armed with the firm knowledge that whatever weather at my point of departure caused me to don the clothing in which I am presently dressed will have left me completely ill-equipped for whatever climatic conditions will prevail during my 70-minute tenure in the taxi line.

At last, in the taxi, I begin what is reputed to be the most dangerous part of my journey. I know, because I have heard the claim innumerable times from otherwise reputable sources, that planes are safer than cars. Yet I cannot shake the impression that I have just escaped from a dangerous flying engine of death and that I have confronted a consumption experience somewhere between a roller coaster ride and a concentration camp. As the taxi lurches toward my hotel, a wave of relief and gratitude passes over me. I feel relieved to put the torments of aerologic and planespeak behind me for at least another day or two and grateful to have arrived safely at my destination. In a sense, that is all that matters now. Aeronautic agonies are just part of the price I pay to be free.

Holbrook's description of air travel is an example of *introspective phenomenology*: a first person account of the researcher's interaction with a consumption phenomenon. In this case, the experience involved flying. Phenomenological inquiry may also concern itself with third person accounts of others' consumption experiences. These occur when a researcher-interpreter uses transcripts of others' recollected consumption experiences to construct an interpretation of their meaning. A recent article by Thompson and colleagues (1990) provides an example of this second type of phenomenological inquiry.

In the partial transcript of an interview presented, a female consumer states: "I went to [a store] the other day to get a brick light, but I asked them about a dimmer, and well, with the hustle bustle of the kids, I got the dimmer and forgot about the brick light. I had to go back and get a brick light. When I got there, they gave me the wrong size brick light . . ." (p. 348). Thompson and colleagues (1990) interweave this example with others the consumer provided about similarly frustrating shopping trips to construct an interpretation of these consumption experiences as creating an uncomfortable sense of indeterminacy in this consumer's life. "Rather than closure, Samantha experienced a frustrating repetition of effort and a troubling awareness of an unfinished task whose final outcome was indeterminate" (p. 348).

Thompson and colleagues (1989, 1990) provide an extensive set of criteria for evaluating the quality of phenomenological research. These are also discussed at length in a monograph by McCracken (1988), which is highly recommended for those who are initiating research in this area.

EXISTENTIALIST STRATEGIES

A second, more radical, existential version of person-centered interpretation characterizes some work by the so-called "new" new critics (Hawkes, 1977, p. 156), the Tel Quel theorists (Culler, 1975, p. 247), the Deconstructionists such as Derrida (Hekman, 1986, p. 195), and the later Roland Barthes (Hawkes, 1977,

p. 115; Kurzweil, 1980, p. 181; Lentricchia, 1980, p. 143). For example, in an oft-cited passage, Barthes (1977) argues for the acceptance of what Hunt (1983) or Muncy and Fisk (1987) would consider radical relativism: the rejection of the relevance of external meaning structures and the celebration of the individual's subjective interpretation.

> A text is made of multiple writings, drawn from many cultures . . . but there is one place where this multiplicity is focused and that place is the reader, and not the author. . . . A text's unity lies not in its origin but in its destination. . . . The birth of the Reader must be at the cost of the death of the Author. (p. 148)

Like some consumer researchers (e.g., Hunt, 1983; Calder & Tybout, 1987, 1989), some philosophers have expressed concern over existentialist-based interpretive strategies. Seung (1982), for example, suggests that such inquiries must inevitably collapse into "textual solipsism":

> Each reader has his or her own version of textual meaning shared by no other, because it is a unique function of that person's psychological conditions. . . . Everyone is trapped in a private world of perception and interpretation. Hence, in the world of solipsism, one cannot even talk of validity . . . except for the world of one's private experience. (p. 198)

However, these fears of existentialist interpretation as autistic science may be overdrawn. Both Sartre and Heidegger acknowledged the centrality of society and interpersonal interaction to the generation of self-identity and personal meaning. Humans, researchers or otherwise, do not function or form interpretations in a vacuum. Inevitably, we possess common meaning structures either socialized from without or generated from within. We cannot escape the similarities of our personal texts with those of others who form an interpretive community (Bruner, 1986, p. 156; Lentricchia, 1980, p. 146). Thus, Fish (1980) notes that even our attempts to create radical interpretations must implicitly embody tacit aspects of the existing structures against which we rebel.

> Rhetorically the new position announces itself as a break from the old, but in fact it is radically dependent on the old, because it is only in the context of some differential relationship that it can be perceived as new, or for that matter, perceived at all (p. 349). . . . That is why the fear of interpretation that is anarchic or totally relativistic will never be realized; for in the event that a fringe or off-the-wall interpretation makes its way into the center, it will merely take its place in a new realignment in which other interpretations will occupy the position of being off-the-wall. That is, off-the-wallness is not a property of interpretations that have been judged inaccurate with respect to a free-standing text, but rather a property of an interpretive system within whose confines the meaning of the text is continually being established and re-established. . . . The further conclusion is that off-the-wallness is not inimical to the system but essential to it and its operation. The production and perception of off-the-wall interpretations is no less a learned and conventional activity, than the production and perception of interpretations that are judged to be acceptable. (pp. 350-351)

Like phenomenological accounts, existential interpretations have appeared only rarely in the consumer-behavior literature, no doubt because of their dialectic stance with respect to traditional neopositivistic science. However, one such research effort based on the Individual Construction of Reality relates the introspective experiences of a self-described member of the consumer-behavior "fringe" (Holbrook, 1986):

> The sudden total eclipse of jazz in my life, the consciousness raised by impending fatherhood, the agony of the Vietnam Era, and deep doubts about whether it was hip to pursue an MBA career produced two momentous consequences—first, a decision to enter Columbia's Ph.D. program in marketing and, second, an embarrassing regression in my musical tastes. I clung to what little security I could find, sought safety in numbers, and began listening to the Stones, the Who, Traffic, Cream, Simon and Garfunkel, Jefferson Airplane, and—yes—even the Beatles. . . . When the rumor started that Paul was dead, I was as concerned as their most loyal

fan. Soon the group itself had perished and I had to look elsewhere for musical sustenance. Thus does hipness founder when it crashes against the rocky shores of the Principle of Irony. (p. 616)

Here, as Fish suggested, we find that this act of subjective self-interpretation is itself structured according to conventional academic norms. Even as it strives to break new ground, it must rely on the existence of consensually constructed and commonly shared structures of meaning (e.g., fatherhood, antimilitarism, the Beatles).

PSYCHOANALYTIC STRATEGIES

In contrast to phenomenology and existentialism, a third approach based on the Individual Construction of Reality does have a history of application in consumer research. Here, we refer to the psychoanalytic perspective associated, above all, with the name Freud (1977). In the 1940s and 1950s, this perspective informed the efforts of the Motivation Researchers (e.g., Dichter, 1960). Now, with the emergence of a new openness to interpretivism, the psychoanalytic perspective appears ripe for revival (old prejudices notwithstanding).

As the locus classicus for the psychoanalytic viewpoint, we might select Freud's (1965b) *The Interpretation of Dreams,* a book that vividly indicates how one's personally constructed narratives provide texts interpretable in terms of their hidden meanings. Briefly, Freud (1965b) suggests that the manifest content of a dream, its surface meaning, disguises a latent content, its hidden meaning, as part of a mechanism that represses forbidden wishes and prevents them from reaching consciousness, but permits their fulfillment in a distorted symbolic form:

The meaning of every dream is the fulfillment of a wish. . . . My theory is not based on a consideration of the manifest content of dreams but refers to the thoughts which are shown by the work of interpretation to lie behind dreams. We must make a contrast between the manifest and the latent content of dreams. . . . Let us describe this behaviour of dreams, which stands in so much need of explanation, as "the phenomena of distortion in dreams." (pp. 167-169)

Freud's approach has received its fair share of criticism (e.g., Fisher & Greenberg, 1985), especially from those unfriendly to postpositivistic perspectives (e.g., Grünbaum, 1984). (For a recent example in consumer research, see Calder & Tybout, 1987.) However, psychoanalysis has also been defended as a penetrating method of systematic self-reflection (Habermas, 1971; Ricoeur, 1981). This defense makes use of the previously discussed arguments for the validity of the Hermeneutic Circle. From this perspective, we may view psychoanalysis as a self-corrective process of interpreting the text of one's own life so as to put one in touch with one's own unconscious wants, desires, and motives. Indeed, we know of no more rigorous approach to the problem of understanding one's own Individual Construction of Reality.

In literary analysis, the psychoanalytic approach has appeared in the work of such critics as Norman Holland (1973). Holland's perspective, as one might expect, treats the literary text as manifest content to be probed for its latent meanings.

> Creative writing, like any other act . . . satisfies . . . some combination of pleasure-giving and defensive needs, inner inertia and outer pressures to change, personal demands and society's stringencies (p. 57). . . . One . . . uses a body of specialized knowledge like psychoanalytic psychology as a way into the encounter. For me, that means using it, for example, to discover relationships between seemingly unrelated parts of the work. One can also discover the ways in which the text represents a transformation of fantasy materials by means of adaptive and defensive strategies for the writer or for the reader. And, too, one can find some of the less obvious connections between the work and particular details and events in the author's life. (pp. 135-136)

Such "less obvious connections" have received increased attention from consumer-behavior researchers. An exception is the self-analysis conducted by Holbrook (1988) entitled "The

Psychoanalytic Interpretation of Consumer Behavior: I am an Animal." This work is of special interest because its author uses a *psychoanalytic* interpretive approach to question an *ethnographic* interpretation rendered by two members of the aforementioned Consumer-Behavior Odyssey. The Odyssey members, after examining several animal theme art objects plus an arsenal of pesticides and insecticides in Holbrook's weekend house, came to the conclusion that they represented the theme "Morris-as-Big-Game-Hunter." That is, that they suggested Holbrook's desire for the destruction of animals and wildlife.

Questioning this interpretation and calling upon images from his childhood, Holbrook (1988) develops an alternative interpretation of these art objects, and others in his possession, as expressing the resolution of Oedipal conflicts experienced during infancy and associated with a phobia related to *Peter and the Wolf*:

> We know that guilt . . . causes us to anticipate some punishment and that, faced with Oedipal longings, the male child tends to develop unconscious fears of castration at the hands of the father. The endangerment of Peter (a clear phallic reference) by the wolf (a clear association with . . . father) fit all too tightly into this overdetermined pattern of latent mental connections. The phobia appears as a clear manifest reflection of these unconscious thoughts. . . . This pattern of latent associations has penetrated into many corners of my psychic world where I shall not invite the reader to wander. Its clear relevance here depends on its connections with artistic objects in our Pennsylvania home. (pp. 165-166)

To validate this interpretation, Holbrook (1988) presents supportive material in the form of (a) other recalled childhood images, (b) further descriptions of current art objects in his New York City residence, and (c) corroborative testimony from his own and another psychoanalyst. The key point that emerges is that psychoanalytic inquiry may lead to interpretations that differ from those of an ethnographic nature, because psychoanalytic approaches provide access to a source of meaning generally inaccessible to the ethnographer: the consumer's unconscious images and feelings. This example demonstrates, as well, that the same cultural text may be "read" differently, depending upon the interpretive vantage point of the researcher.

SUGGESTED READING

Iser, W. (1978). *The act of reading.* Baltimore, MD: Johns Hopkins University Press.

McCracken, G. (1988). *The long interview.* Newbury Park, CA: Sage.

➤ PART THREE ◄

EVALUATING RESEARCH

13

BE GENTLE
WITH THE TEXT

In this book, we have proposed a worldview in which different ways of approaching different truths can exist side by
side. We advocate an acceptance of the acknowledgement
that perspectives varying between the extremes of Material and
Mental Determinism can all attain high levels of internal coher-
ence and external relevance to the various realities constructed
by interpretive communities. As Geertz (1983) notes:

> We more and more see ourselves surrounded by a vast, almost
> continuous field of variously intended and diversely constructed
> works [that] we can order practically, relationally and as our purposes
> prompt us. . . . Scientists have become free to shape their work in terms
> of their necessities, rather than according to received ideas as to what
> they ought or ought not to be doing. (pp. 20-21)

Our present effort has been directed toward assisting consumer researchers to make those choices in an informed and

personally comfortable manner. As Morgan and Smircich (1980) observe, "the choice and adequacy of a method embody a variety of assumptions regarding the nature of knowledge and the methods through which that knowledge can be obtained" (p. 491). Researchers must decide for themselves what assumptions about reality they will embrace and then follow the research strategies appropriate to those assumptions. Consumer research inquiry, in this sense, is very much an act of faith; research practices, like religious practices, must spring from that faith.

The key to appreciating this ecumenical perspective lies in viewing the researcher's subject as a text and the researcher's task as one of interpretation. On this theme, the instructor for a course in hermeneutics attended by one of the authors concluded his final lecture with the following piece of advice: "When all is said and done, *be gentle with the text*." To this plea for interpretive humility, we can only add a wish for mutual tolerance: "Be gentle with the text and be gentle with *each other*." Do not reject another researcher's work merely because it stems from an epistemology at variance with your own. Remember that Plato, Aristotle, Descartes, Locke, Hume, Marx, Kant, Husserl, Sartre, and the others sprang from very different philosophical roots and established contrasting perspectives that still coexist today. Indeed, the ideas of these philosophers will likely endure long past the time when the epistemic issues of current concern to consumer-behavior research have ceased to matter.

So, in humility, "be gentle with the text and be gentle with each other." Those words are easy to say and tempt us to end on this note of comfort. But, however reassuring these words may sound, they fail to describe the state of affairs that actually prevails in consumer research today, especially that which manifests itself in the rejoinders that we address to one another and in the review process that occurs at our major journals and other homes for scholarly publications. These avenues for commentary and criticism are often characterized, we believe, by the kind of internecine hostility that Schweder (1984) has described as typical of the social sciences in general:

> Experts in the social sciences tend to be territorial, staking out for themselves one small cell in a larger matrix of possibilities. For many social theorists, staking is followed by imperialistic expansionism—the ambitious attempt to expand one's cell to include the whole matrix. . . . For other social theorists, staking is followed by fortification and boundary maintenance: the inglorious attempt to wall out anything not in one's cell, to ignore or even taboo all alien phenomena. (pp. 58-59)

We believe that the kind of intellectual territoriality noted by Schweder in the social sciences generally applies conspicuously to the case of consumer research. We also believe that the growth of knowledge in our discipline can flourish only when such potential hostilities have given way to some form of peaceful coexistence. Toward that end, we shall devote the remainder of this concluding chapter to describing and, we hope, clarifying the nature of the conflicts that trouble the waters of consumer research at the present time.

THE PROBLEM

However regrettable it may seem to those with tender hearts, warfare rages today among scholars and scientists in the field of consumer research. Members of opposing camps fight this combat with figurative instead of literal weapons, with manuscripts instead of guns, with words instead of ammunition. The terrain each seeks to capture lies at the center of knowledge in our discipline. The battle for dominance over this intellectual turf—though less bloody and less deadly—proceeds as stubbornly and relentlessly as any armed conflict.

But the battle lines for this war among consumer researchers resemble the swamped boundaries, blurred identities, and fuzzy loyalties that characterize a guerrilla warfare that grinds on endlessly without hope of termination, much less resolution. In this, the conflict recalls Vietnam more than World War II. It threatens to sap the strength of its participants without offering any possibility of victory. It promises only waste with no chance of success for the self-proclaimed righteous on various sides of the struggle.

We see the fallout from this war every day in the faces of colleagues mourning the fates of their latest papers. We hear it in the acrimonious tones of debates among committee members grappling with their responsibilities for life-and-death tenure cases and other promotion decisions. We smell it in the unctuous self-righteousness of the reviews that guide the editorial processes at our leading journals. We taste it in the aftermath of rejections too painful to bear. We feel it in our deep sense of outrage over what "they" are doing to "us." (If the reader does not experience these sights, sounds, smells, tastes, and feelings, he or she is encouraged to take a sober look at his or her file of rejections and papers under revision.)

We hate war. We hated it in Vietnam. And we hate it when it defoliates, depopulates, and demolishes the field to which we have chosen to devote our intellectual energies. We hate it when it pits friend against friend, when we watch it break hearts and ruin careers, and when we realize with a growing sense of despair that, as a community of scholars, consumer researchers do not seem to understand it, to recognize its dangers, or to entertain any coherent notions of how to stop it before *it* does enough further irreparable damage to stop *us.*

Much as we hate this intellectual warfare in consumer research, we make no claim that we know how to end it. Indeed, none of us can resolve what we fail to understand. And we believe that consumer researchers do fail to understand the battles that rage in our discipline. Further, we suspect that our colleagues can hope to achieve a peace with honor—though, inevitably, a peace without victory—only if we can begin to articulate the nature of the conflict that surrounds us. Toward that end, we shall offer one view of the multidimensional divisions that bring discord and dissonance to the field of consumer research. We hope thereby to kindle a tiny flicker of light, a glimpse of clarity, to illuminate and penetrate that murky morass of dissension in which we all seem to struggle endlessly.

PURPOSE, PHILOSOPHY, PERSPECTIVE, AND PERSONALITY

Toward the goal of clarifying the intellectual conflict that surrounds the work of scholars in consumer behavior, we suggest that commentary and criticism in the field of consumer research—by which we refer primarily to the signed rejoinders that appear in print and the anonymous reviews that support editorial decisions concerning the publishability of manuscripts at our leading journals—rest on four basic types of underpinnings that provide their axiological, conceptual, and methodological support. Mimicking McCarthy (1971), who organized the primary elements of the marketing mix into his famous set of four "Ps" (product, price, place, and promotion), we shall designate the "Four Key Bases for Commentary and Criticism in Consumer Research" by four terms that also begin with the letter "P": Purpose, Philosophy of Science, Perspective, and Personality. Further, as shown in Figure 13.1, we shall characterize each basis (each "P") by a dichotomy or continuum represented by two extreme positions that might describe any given approach to commentary or criticism. Technically, each of the distinctions drawn in Figure 13.1 represents a range between polar opposites with various intermediate positions or gray areas in between. It will simplify the discussion if we treat these as straightforward contrasts rather than as graduated dimensions. However, the reader should keep in mind the proviso that we intend to describe a multidimensional space rather than a set of tight logical categories (as would be implied, for example, by the cells of a $2 \times 2 \times 2$ matrix). Having issued this disclaimer, we shall discuss in more detail each basis shown in Figure 13.1 and the distinction on which it rests.

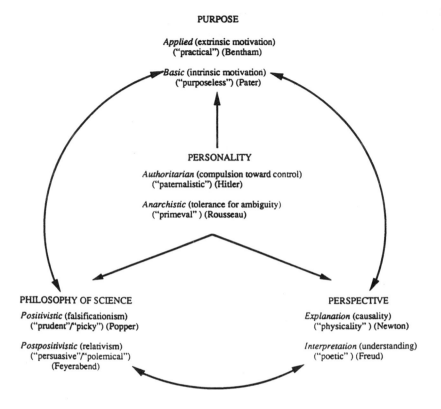

Figure 13.1. Four Key Bases for Commentary and Criticism in Consumer Research

PURPOSE

We use the term *Purpose* to designate the reasons assumed in a commentary or critical review as the justification for a piece of research. Here, we may distinguish between *applied* and *basic* orientations (e.g., Langfitt, Hackney, Fishman, & Glowasky, 1983; Myers, Massy, & Greyser, 1980). These differ according to whether they proceed from *extrinsic* or *intrinsic* motivation (e.g., Hagstrom, 1965; Hyde, 1983). The former type of motivational orientation views consumer research as a means to the end of improving managerial decision making; the latter sees it as an end in itself directed toward creating knowledge for its own sake and for no other external purpose. (For reviews of this difference in scholarship, with several relevant references, see Hirschman, 1987b; Holbrook, 1989.)

Colloquially, we might distinguish the motivational stances implied by applied (extrinsically motivated) versus basic (intrinsically motivated) research as "practical" versus "purposeless" (words chosen for their mnemonic value by virtue of the fact that they, too, begin with the letter "P"). Typical thinkers that illustrate this contrast in our Western culture would include, Jeremy Bentham, the arch-utilitarian, as opposed to Walter Pater, a father of aestheticism.

PHILOSOPHY OF SCIENCE

At the risk of oversimplification, we shall characterize the *Philosophy of Science* adopted in a given piece of commentary or criticism as leaning toward one of two poles that we shall label *positivistic* and *postpositivistic*, respectively. By positivistic, we refer primarily to the viewpoints and procedures that typify the hypothetico-deductive method (e.g., hypothesis formulation, measurement operationalization, experimental or other empirical testing, statistical inference, etc.), as supported by most advocates of approaches akin to logical empiricism or other versions of the received view (e.g., Calder & Tybout, 1987; Hunt, 1983). By postpositivism, we refer to the host of questions and alternative conceptions of science raised and proposed by those postmodernists (Sherry, 1991) who challenge the epistemological grounds for neopositivism by substituting new standards of plausibility or trustworthiness for the old criteria of validity (e.g., Anderson, 1983, 1986; Hirschman, 1986; Hudson & Ozanne, 1988; Peter & Olson, 1983; and many other SCR, LCR, ICR, or MCR thinkers described earlier in this book).

Without wishing to inflame or even to encourage this already heated debate in the present context, we might vernacularly label the positions espoused by these opposing philosophical camps by such P-words as "prudent" (sometimes verging on "picky") versus "persuasive" (sometimes verging on "polemical"), respectively. Great thinkers admired by the two contrasting schools of thought would include Sir Karl Popper, champion of falsificationism, as opposed to Paul Feyerabend, prophet of relativism.

PERSPECTIVE

The *Perspective* that guides the evaluation of consumer research mirrors the aforementioned differences drawn by Dilthey between the Natural Sciences (Naturwissenschaften) and the Human Studies (Geisteswissenschaften) (Makkreel, 1975). Like any social science, extrapolating from the arguments of Harré and Secord (1973), studies of consumer behavior might lean toward either perspective. The former emphasizes explanation via the formulation of models intended to account for the causality underlying some phenomenon or fundamental to some text of interest. The latter stresses interpretation through the understanding of what some event or text means to the creators or actors engaged in producing or consuming it. (For a good discussion of this difference in emphasis, see Ricoeur, 1976.)

In everyday terms, causal explanation differs from interpretive understanding in something like the way that the deterministic mechanics of classical physics (the Universe as text) differ from the figurative and multilayered meanings of poetry (the Word as text). Or, to preserve our emphasis on the letter "P," the manner that "physicalistic" differs from "poetic." Great proponents of these competing orientations would include Sir Isaac Newton, paragon of Enlightenment physics, as opposed to Sigmund Freud, whose scientistic pretensions could not undermine the essentially interpretive thrust in his analysis of dreams, artworks, and other human behavioral artifacts.

PERSONALITY

Finally, the *Personality* implied by the evaluative stance adopted in a particular piece of commentary or criticism reflects a psychodynamic orientation that might range from an extreme authoritarianism bordering on a compulsion toward control to the elevated tolerance for ambiguity typical of anarchists. Here, we use *authoritarian*, in the sense conveyed by the "F"-for-"Fascism" Scale (Adorno, et al., 1982), to designate a tendency to seek order, to follow rules, and to accept or impose strong, even autocratic or dictatorial, conventions of obedience. By contrast, we use *anarchistic* to indicate a preference for lawlessness, disorder, inappropriateness, tension, disorientation, or chaos, as found in certain extreme romantics (Peckham, 1965).

Few would doubt that personalities of both types characterize many of the reviews that guide editorial decisions at our major journals of marketing and consumer behavior. (Indeed, some writers—the present authors included, perhaps—may display "multiple personalities" by shifting their positions from one occasion to the next along the range between authoritarianism and anarchism.) On the one hand, reminiscent of Milgram's (1975) obedient subjects who continued to administer what they thought were excruciatingly painful electric shocks to their ostensible victims, we have those "paternalistic" pieces of criticism that stubbornly adhere to the most elitist, exclusionary, and self-righteous standards of evaluation, oblivious to the suffering thereby inflicted on the prospective authors who desperately seek apparently unattainable approval. On the other hand, displaying a militant iconoclasm that borders on an indifference to reality, we find those specimens of "primeval" permissiveness that flout all standards of intellectual decorum, substituting capricious criteria based on wayward irresponsibility or even paroxysms of self-indulgence. (Admittedly, to reiterate a point emphasized earlier, some examples of commentary and criticism do manage to fall between these two poles of the continuum, though perhaps fewer than one might wish.) Historical analogies to these extreme postures, by which we intend nothing more than a simple mnemonic for keeping the differences clearly in mind, might include Hitler, the proverbial proto-Fascist, in contrast to Rousseau, who glorified the noble savage in an idealized primitive state of nature.

PROPOSITIONS

In sum, it seems reasonable to characterize the commentary and criticism that appear in the field of consumer behavior as resting on four basic dimensions: Purpose, Philosophy of Science, Perspective, and Personality. Each reflects a fundamental contrast between two polar extremes: applied/basic, positivistic/postpositivistic, explanatory/interpretive, and authoritarian/anarchistic, respectively. With this framework in mind, we can now entertain two propositions that provide additional content to the scheme portrayed in Figure 13.1. To preview briefly, we shall argue that the four key bases for commentary and criticism in consumer research are (a) conceptually distinct and (b) empirically related. These points enrich our understanding of the evaluative process by introducing fifth and sixth "P"-concepts to our version of the "Four Ps": Potentialities and Propensities. We shall argue for the differences between Potentialities and Propensities by means of Propositions I and II, to which we now turn.

(I) Proposition Concerning Potentialities: The Four Ps Are Conceptually Distinct

As a first proposition, we suggest that, conceptually, the Four Ps shown in Figure 13.1 are distinct. (For a related point, see Schweder, 1984, p. 60.) In other words, no logical reason exists to rule out any position in the proposed four-dimensional space (or any of the sixteen possible combinations based on the four pairs of extreme orientations).

Thus, for example, an applied research purpose could coexist with a post- or nonpositivistic philosophy of science; indeed, one suspects that most managerial marketing practitioners adopt just such a combined orientation (many of them, perhaps, implicitly or unintentionally). Similarly, the most neopositivistic research could pursue interpretive understanding in the meaning of some text or event. Here, as noted earlier, the possibility of applying falsificationist criteria of validity constitutes one of the few points of agreement between Hirsch (1967) and Ricoeur (1976). Again, one seeking explanation according to a model of causality could proceed from the vantage point of anarchism; thus, for example, Feyerabend (1975) proclaimed that "anything goes" in direct connection with considerations drawn from the context of the physical sciences as pertaining to what we might call the Text or Book of Nature. Finally, an authoritarian might adopt a motivational orientation consistent with basic research. Perhaps, in this sense, a few of Hitler's doctors might have entertained some macabre but purely intellectual curiosity concerning the outcomes of the horrific medical "experiments" performed in the Nazi concentration camps.

All this demonstrates that, both in studies of consumer behavior and in the broader sphere of scientific research in general, no necessary logical connection links variations along the continua that characterize Purpose, Philosophy of Science, Perspective, and Personality. In this sense, the potential exists for any combination of the four Ps to occur.

(II) Proposition Concerning Propensities: The Four Ps Are Empirically Related

However, as a second proposition anticipated implicitly throughout much of this book, we believe that the four Ps shown in Figure 13.1 tend to be related empirically. In other words, though they have the *potential* to vary independently and are therefore conceptually distinct (Proposition I), they have a *propensity* to vary together in a manner that renders them empirically related in practice (Proposition II). Here, we suspect that the driving force arises from the personality that characterizes the orientation adopted by a particular commentator or critic. Thus, as shown by the single- and double-headed arrows in Figure 13.1, we believe that Personality tends to determine Purpose, Philosophy, and Perspective in such a way that interrelations among the latter three bases also tend to occur.

In general, then, one might hypothesize that, among the rejoinders and reviews attempting to evaluate research on consumer behavior or on consumption as text, authoritarian exemplars might tend to favor applied research that addresses problems relevant to managerial practitioners and that proceeds by the clear rules of neopositivism toward explanation by means of a causal model. Conversely, anarchistic exemplars might tend to prefer basic research via a postpositivistic approach to interpretive understanding.

Such propensities might be relatively strong or weak. At the moment, they exist only as a proposition that itself awaits evaluation (via neopositivistic or postpositivistic methods). The advantage of such a proposition is that, if valid, it would help to explain the otherwise inexplicably rapacious savagery of the rejoinders and reviews by means of which commentators and critics ravage the most sincere efforts by their friends and colleagues in consumer research.

THE PRINCIPLE OF PERVERSITY

Where everything in a commentator's or critic's worldview seems to cohere in a self-reinforcing cycle that confirms the premises underlying that commentator's rejoinder or that confers an impression of infallibility upon that critic's review, the person in question can scarcely avoid the conviction that his or her evaluative judgments rest on intellectual bedrock in such a manner as to render them virtually apodictic. One can hardly expect to find humility in an individual blessed with the attainment of so high an achievement in self-consistency. One might rather expect to encounter rejoinders and reviews written from the vantage point of the most unexampled self-satisfaction.

This effect may help to account for the aforementioned predicament wherein consumer researchers appear to engage in a kind of internecine warfare in which the lines of battle remain unclear, as if submerged in a swamp of conceptual confusion or a morass of muddled rhetoric. Our analysis has argued that this perplexing state of affairs results from not one but four conceptually distinct but empirically related bases for commentary and criticism in research on consumer behavior. Only by understanding this complex of interacting factors that operate in the evaluation of research in our field can consumer researchers hope to guard against the potentially hostile forces arrayed against their work on one or the other side, or even both sides of the parallel distinctions that we have drawn. This, in a sense, is our major conclusion here. It is not astounding, perhaps, but maybe propaedeutic to a fuller understanding of the area in which we operate when we conduct research on consumption as text.

But at another, deeper level, we find ourselves moving in the direction of a more profoundly disturbing conclusion that implies something rather distressing about the springs of conflict in our discipline and the roots for what look like conspicuous symptoms of people's inhumanity toward their fellow creatures and their fruits of labors. At bottom, one must ask why scholars choose to write rejoinders and reviews that purposely degrade the work of their friends and colleagues.

In part, optimistically, one might lay the blame at the feet of a possibly awesome and compelling intellectual integrity that carries all before it in the sweep of its ineluctable quest for truth and beauty. Here, indeed, one might argue that our procedures for evaluating consumer research lead toward the improvement of manuscripts, the purification of academic careers, and the elevation of our collective scholarly output.

At the same time, perhaps more realistically if more offensively to those with high ideals, one might suspect that something essentially nasty creeps within the hearts and minds that most of us bring to the task of creating commentary and criticism. We fear that this somewhat cynical or even sinister streak threatens to taint the critical faculties of all those who labor in the vineyards of knowledge surrounding the field of consumer research. In short—in speaking of an insidious ailment that, in spite of ourselves and our purported desire to build a kinder and gentler discipline, tends to undermine our best efforts at scholarship—we speak of Everyman.

In conducting a study and writing a paper, an author performs a creative act. Essentially, it is an act of love. One might think that readers would react appreciatively and would respond with positive comments or constructive criticisms or maybe even sincere praise. One might hope that we would approach each other's work in the spirit of humility, helpfulness, and humanity. One might expect to find compassion in our attempts to evaluate one another. Yet, all too often, it does not work that way.

Samuel Taylor Coleridge and Edgar Allen Poe understood such things. Here, we are reminded of an essay in which Stanley Cavell (1986) considers Coleridge's *The Rime of the Ancient Mariner* and asks *why*, for what motive, the Mariner shot the Albatross. Cavell suggests that he killed the bird because it loved him and that "the killing is to be understood as the denial of some claim upon him" (p. 193). In this, Cavell restates the conventional interpretation of the poem's moral as "to let yourself *be loved* by all things both great and small" (pp. 193-194).

Too often, as consumer researchers committed to the creation of our own work and the evaluation of work by others, we forget these basic conditions of humanity. We picture ourselves as embarked on some kind of intellectual voyage in which all temptations toward human kindness, all temptations toward simple acts of humility and helpfulness, compassion and friendship, must be avoided lest they thwart our ceaseless efforts to seek a new Kingdom of Knowledge. Thus, Odysseus must leave Kalypso; Aeneas must abandon Dido; Faust must surrender Gretchen; the Argonauts must continue their quest without tethering themselves for long to the human ties that bind. And if, on this journey, we must sacrifice an albatross or two along the way? Well, such evil side effects have been the price of knowledge ever since the Fall. We should not expect merely mortal scholars to resist what not even God Himself would prevent.

But, here, Cavell introduces a chilling parallel with Poe's story, "The Black Cat." In this frightening tale, doubly distressing to anyone who identifies with the feline temperament, the narrator kills his cat because he knows that the cat loves him. In this, he consummates his subjugation to a force that he calls the "spirit of Perverseness":

> And then came, as if my final and irrevocable overthrow, the spirit of Perverseness. . . . It was this unfathomable longing of the soul *to vex itself*—to offer violence to its own nature—to do wrong for the wrong's sake only—that urged me to continue and finally to consummate the injury I had inflicted upon the unoffending brute. One morning, in cold blood, I slipped a noose about its neck and hung it to the limb of a tree;—hung it with the tears streaming from my eyes, and with the bitterest remorse at my heart;—hung it *because* I knew that in so doing I was committing a sin. (quoted by Cavell, 1986, pp. 214-215)

We fear that something like this "spirit of Perverseness," this Principle of Perversity, threatens to infect us all every time we pick up a pen to write some commentary or criticism, ready to sit in merciless judgment of work by a friend, colleague, or fellow scholar. Pray that we learn to resist it before it foments a state of unremitting intellectual hostility from which our field of study might never recover.

PRAYER

- Let us treat our colleagues and their labors of love gently, remembering the enormous care and toil that they have invested in even the most seemingly small piece of research.

- Let us be kind to those who contribute their scholarly efforts as an offering intended to bring light and, perhaps, joy into the world. Remember always the central theme of this book, that multiple viewpoints with different but equally valid claims to truth and beauty exist as alternative bases upon which to conduct consumer research.

- Let us resist the temptation to tie ourselves up into self-consistent knots in which extreme but mutually reinforcing personality driven positions on Purpose, Philosophy of Science, and Perspective serve to bolster self-righteous condemnations of work conducted from the vantage point of some other worldview.

- Let us pursue the neglected virtues of humility, helpfulness, and humanity and honor the prophetic vision articulated by Kenneth Burke (1969) when he reminded us that "there are objections to any position": "You can even attack a thing on the grounds that it is exactly what it claims to be" (pp. 97-98).

- Let us respond to this realization by maintaining flexible, inquisitive, resilient minds and by acknowledging the mutual coexistence of potentially contradictory research paradigms.

- Let us celebrate the proliferation of truths from innumerable perspectives on the nature of consumer behavior and the meanings of consumption as text.

- And let us accept this broadened appreciation for the pluralistic richness of knowledge in our field as the foundation for an embrace of the most glorious of all P-words in our language. The one toward which all thought, all feeling, and ultimately all scholarship should aspire: PEACE.

REFERENCES

Adorno, T. W., Frenkel-Brunswik, E., Levinson, D. J., & Sanford, R. N. (1982). *The authoritarian personality*. New York: Norton.

Althusser, L. (1971). *Lenin and philosophy*. London: New Left Books.

Althusser, L. (1972a). *For Marx*. New York: Pantheon.

Althusser, L. (1972b). *Politics and History*. London: New Left Books.

Anderson, P. F. (1983, Fall). Marketing, scientific progress and scientific method. *Journal of Marketing, 47*, 18-31.

Anderson, P. F. (1986, September). On method in consumer research: A critical relativist perspective. *Journal of Consumer Research, 13*, 155-173.

Anderson, P. F. (1989). On Relativism and interpretivism—with a prolegomenon to the 'Why' question. In E. C. Hirschman (Ed.), *Interpretive consumer Research* (pp. 10-23). Provo, UT: Association for Consumer Research.

Arnould, E. J. (1989, September). Toward a broadened theory of preference formation and the diffusion of innovations: Cases from Zinder province, Niger republic. *Journal of Consumer Research, 16*, 239-267.

Ayer, A. J. (1956). *The problem of knowledge*. Harmondsworth, England: Penguin.

Ayer, A. J. (1980). *Hume*. New York: Hill and Wang.

Baltzell, E. D. (1964). *The Protestant establishment: Aristocracy and caste in America*. New York: Vintage.

Barthes, R. (1967). *Elements of semiology*. (A. Lavers & C. Smith, Trans.) New York: Hill and Wang.

Barthes, R. (1972). *Mythologies*. London: Jonathan Cape.

Barthes, R. (1974). *S/Z*. (R. Miller, Trans.) New York: Hill and Wang.

Barthes, R. (1977). The death of the author. In R. Barthes (Ed.), *Image-music-text*. Glasgow: Fontana-Collins.

Barthes, R. (1983). *The fashion system* (M. Ward & R. Howard, Trans.). New York: Hill and Wang.

Belk, R. W., Sherry, J. F., Jr., & Wallendorf, M. (1988, March). A naturalistic inquiry into buyer and seller behavior at a swap meet. *Journal of Consumer Research, 14*, 449-470.

Belk, R. W., Wallendorf, M., & Sherry, J. F. (1989, June). The sacred and profane in consumer behavior: Theodicy on the Odyssey. *Journal of Consumer Research, 16*, 1-38.

Berger, P. L., & Luckmann, T. (1966). *The social construction of reality*. New York: Doubleday.

Berkeley, G. (1974). A treatise concerning the principle of human knowledge. In *The empiricists* (pp. 135-215) Garden City, NY: Anchor Books.

Berlyne, D. E. (1971). *Aesthetics and psychobiology*. New York: Appleton-Century-Crofts.

Berlyne, D. E. (Ed.). (1974). *Studies in the new experimental esthetics*. New York: John Wiley.

Bernstein, R. J. (1983). *Beyond objectivism and relativism: Science, hermeneutics, and praxis*. Philadelphia: University of Pennsylvania Press.

Bernstein, R. J. (1985). *Beyond objectivism and relativism: Science, hermeneutics, and praxis*. Philadelphia: University of Pennsylvania Press.

Bettman, J. (1979). *An information processing theory of consumer choice*. Reading, MA: Addison-Wesley.

Bleicher, J. (1980). *Contemporary hermeneutics: Hermeneutics as method, philosophy and critique*. London: Routledge & Kegan Paul.

Bleicher, J. (1982). *The hermeneutic imagination: Outline of a positive critique of scientism and sociology*. London: Routledge & Kegan Paul.

Bloor, D. (1983). *Wittgenstein: A social theory of knowledge*. New York: Columbia University Press.

Bruner, J. (1986). *Actual minds, possible worlds*. Cambridge, MA: Harvard University Press.

Brunswik, E. (1943). Organismic achievement and environmental probability. *Psychological Review, 50*, 255-272.

Brunswik, E. (1955). Representative design and probabilistic theory in a functional psychology. *Psychological Review, 62*, 193-217.

Brunswik, E. (1956). *Perception and representative design of psychological experiments*. Berkeley: University of California Press.

Burke, K. (1969). *A rhetoric of motives*. Berkeley: University of California Press.

Burke, P. V. (1985). *Vico*. Oxford: Oxford University Press.

Calder, B. J., & Tybout, A. M. (1987, June). What consumer research is. . . . *Journal of Consumer Research, 14*, 136-140.

Calder, B. J., & Tybout, A. M. (1989). Interpretive, qualitative, and traditional scientific empirical consumer behavior research. In E. C. Hirschman (Ed.), *Interpretive Consumer Research* (pp. 199-208). Provo, UT: Association for Consumer Research.

Campbell, K. (1984). *Body and mind*. Notre Dame, IL: University of Notre Dame Press.

Cavell, S. (1986). In quest of the ordinary: Texts of recovery. In M. Eaves & M. Fischer (Eds.), *Romanticism and contemporary criticism* (pp. 183-239). Ithaca, NY: Cornell University Press.

Cawelti, J. G. (1976). *Adventure mystery and romance: Formula stories as art and popular culture*. Chicago: University of Chicago Press.

Chomsky, N. (1965). *Aspects of a theory of syntax*. Cambridge, MA: MIT.

Culler, J. (1975). *Structuralist poetics*. Ithaca, NY: Cornell University Press.

Descartes, R. (1986). *Meditations on first philosophy* (J. Cottingham, Trans.). Cambridge: Cambridge University Press.

Deshpande, R. (1983, Fall). Paradigms lost: On theory and method in research in marketing. *Journal of Marketing, 47*, 101-110.

Dichter, E. (1960). *The strategy of desire*. New York: Doubleday.

Dilthey, W. (1972). The rise of hermeneutics. *New Literary History* (F. Jameson, Trans.), *3*, 229-244.

Eagleton, T. (1983). *Literary theory*. Minneapolis: University of Minnesota Press.

Eco, U. (1973). *Das offere kunstiverk* (G. Memmert, Trans.). Frankfurt.

Eco, U. (1976). *A theory of semiotics*. Bloomington: Indiana University Press.

Eco, U. (1979). *The role of the reader: Explorations in the semiotics of texts*. Bloomington: Indiana University Press.

Empson, W. (1949). *Seven types of ambiguity*. New York. New Directions.

Farrell, T. B. (1985, Autumn). Narrative in natural discourse: On conversation and rhetoric. *Journal of Communication, 35*, 109-127.

Fennell, G. (1985). Things of heaven and earth: Phenomenology, marketing, and consumer research. In E. C. Hirschman & M. B. Holbrook (Eds.), *Advances in consumer research* (Vol. 12, pp. 544-549). Provo, UT: Association for Consumer Research.

Feyerabend, P. (1975). *Against method: Outline of an anarchistic's theory of knowledge*. London: Verso.

Fish, S. (1976). Interpreting the variorum. *Critical Inquiry, 2*, 478.

Fish, S. (1980). *Is there a text in this class: The authority of interpretive communities*. Cambridge, MA: Harvard University Press.

Fisher, S., & Greenberg, R. P. (1985). *The scientific credibility of Freud's theories and therapy*. New York: Columbia University Press.

Fisher, W. R. (1985, Autumn). The narrative paradigm: In the beginning. *Journal of Communication, 35*, 74-89.

Foltz, K. (1989, December 18). New species for study: Consumers in action. *The New York Times*, pp. A1, D10.

Foucault, M. (1965). *Madness and civilization*. New York: Random House.

Foucault, M. (1970). *The order of things*. New York: Pantheon.

Foucault, M. (1973). *The birth of the clinic*. New York: Pantheon.

Foucault, M. (1977). *Discipline and punishment*. New York: Pantheon.

Freud, S. (1965a). *Group psychology and the analysis of the ego* (J. Strachey, Trans.). New York: Norton.

Freud, S. (1965b). *The interpretation of dreams* (J. Strachey, Trans.). New York: Avon Books.

Freud, S. (1977). *Introductory lectures on psychoanalysis* (J. Strachey, Trans.). New York: Norton.

Frye, N. (1957). *Anatomy of criticism*. Princeton, NJ: Princeton University Press.

Gadamer, H. (1974-1975). Hermeneutics and social science. *Cultural Hermeneutics, 2,* 163-181.

Gadamer, H. (1975). *Truth and method.* New York: Crossroad.

Gadamer, H. (1976). *Philosophical hermeneutics.* Berkeley: University of California Press.

Garfinkel, H. (1967). *Studies in ethnomethodology.* Englewood Cliffs, NJ: Prentice-Hall.

Geertz, C. (1973). *The interpretation of cultures.* New York: Basic Books.

Geertz, C. (1983). *Local knowledge: Further essays in interpretive anthropology.* New York: Basic Books.

Geertz, C. (1988). *Works and lives: The anthropologist as author.* Palo Alto, CA: Stanford University Press.

Goldmann, L. (1964). *The hidden god: A study of tragic vision in the Pensees of Pascal and the tragedies of Racine.* London: Routledge & Kegan Paul.

Goldmann, L. (1967a, September 28). Ideology and writing, *Times Literary Supplement.*

Goldmann, L. (1967b). The sociology of literature. *International Social Science Journal, 19*(4).

Goldmann, L. (1969). *The human sciences and philosophy.* London: Jonathan Cape.

Goldmann, L. (1975). *Towards a sociology of the novel.* London: Tavistook.

Griswold, W. (1987, March). The fabrication of meaning: Literary interpretation in the United States, Great Britain and the West Indies. *American Journal of Sociology, 92,* 1077-1117.

Grünbaum, A. (1984). *The foundations of psychoanalysis: A philosophical critique.* Berkeley: University of California Press.

Guiraud, P. (1975). *Semiology* (G. Gross, Trans.). London: Routledge & Kegan Paul.

Habermas, J. (1971). *Knowledge and human interests* (J. J. Shapiro, Trans.). Boston: Beacon Press.

Hagstrom, W. O. (1965). *The scientific community.* Carbondale: Southern Illinois University Press.

Harrari, J. V. (1979). *Textual strategies: Perspectives in post-structuralist criticism.* Ithaca, NY: Cornell University Press.

Harré, R. & Secord, P. F. (1973). *The explanation of social behaviour.* Totowa, NJ: Littlefield, Adams.

Hawkes, T. (1977). *Structuralism and semiotics.* Berkeley: University of California Press.

Hawthorne, J. (1977). Ideology, science and literature. *Marxism Today, 21,* 7-15.

Heidegger, M. (1958). *The question of being* (W. Kluback & J. T. Wilde, Trans.). New York: Twayne.

Heidegger, M. (1962). *Being and time* (J. MacQuarrie & E. S. Robinson, Trans.). New York: Harper and Row.

Heidegger, M. (1968). *What is called thinking* (F. D. Weick & J. G. Gray, Trans.). New York: Harper & Row.

Hekman, S. J. (1986). *Hermeneutics and the sociology of knowledge.* Notre Dame, IL: University of Notre Dame Press.

Hempel, C. G. (1966). *Philosophy of natural science.* Englewood Cliffs, NJ: Prentice-Hall.

Heritage, J. (1984). *Garfinkel and ethnomethodology.* Cambridge: Polity.

Hirsch, E. D., Jr. (1967). *Validity in interpretation.* New Haven, CT: Yale University Press.

Hirsch, E. D., Jr. (1976). *The aims of interpretation.* Chicago: University of Chicago Press.

Hirschman, E. C. (1985). Dual consciousness and altered states: Implications for consumer research. *Journal of Business Research,* Summer, 115-136.

Hirschman, E. C. (1986, August). Humanistic inquiry in marketing research: Philosophy, method, and criteria. *Journal of Marketing Research, 21,* 237-249.

Hirschman, E. C. (1987a). Movies as myths: An interpretation of motion picture mythology. In J. Umiker-Sebeok (Ed.), *Marketing and Semiotics* (pp. 335-376). Berlin: Mouton de Gruyter.

Hirschman, E. C. (1987b). Marketing research: To serve what purpose? In R. W. Belk, et al. (Eds.), *Marketing Theory, proceedings of the AMA Winter Educators' Conference* (pp. 204-208). Chicago: American Marketing Association.

Hirschman, E. C. (1988). *The ideology of consumption: A structural-syntactical analysis of* Dallas *and* Dynasty. *15,* 344-359.

Hirschman, E. C., & Holbrook, M. B. (1982, Summer). Hedonic consumption: Emerging concepts, methods and propositions. *Journal of Marketing, 46,* 92-101.

Hirschman, E. C., & Holbrook, M. B. (1986). Expanding the ontology and methodology of research on the consumption experience. In D. Brinberg & R. Lutz (Eds.), *Methodological innovations in consumer behavior* (pp. 213-251). New York: Springer-Verlag.

Holbrook, M. B. (1981, February). Integrating compositional and decompositional analyses to represent the intervening role of perceptions in evaluative judgments. *Journal of Marketing Research, 18,* 13-28.

Holbrook, M. B. (1986). I'm hip: An autobiographical account of some consumption experiences. In R. Lutz (Ed.), *Advances in consumer research* (Vol. 13, pp. 614-618). Provo, UT: Association for Consumer Research.

Holbrook, M. B. (1987). The study of signs in consumer esthetics: An egocentric review. In J. Umiker-Sebeok, *Marketing and semiotics: New directions in the study of signs for sale* (pp. 73-122). Berlin: Mouton de Gruyter.

Holbrook, M. B. (1988). The psychoanalytic interpretation of consumer behavior. In J. N. Sheth & E. C. Hirschman (Eds.), *Research in consumer behavior,* (Vol. 3, pp. 149-178). Greenwich, CT: JAI.

Holbrook, M. B. (1989, September). Aftermath of the task force: Dogmatism and catastrophe in the development of marketing thought. *ACR Newsletter,* 1-11.

Holbrook, M. B., Bell, S., & Grayson, M. W. (1989). The role of the humanities in consumer research. In E. C. Hirschman (Ed.), *Interpretive consumer research* (pp.29-47). Provo, UT: Association for Consumer Research.

Holbrook, M. B., & Bertges, S. A. (1981). Perceptual veridicality in esthetic communication: A model, general procedure, and illustration. *Communication Research, 8,* 387-424.

Holbrook, M. B., & Grayson, M. W. (1986, December). The semiology of cinematic consumption: Symbolic consumer behavior in *Out of Africa. Journal of Consumer Research, 13,* 374-381.

Holbrook, M. B., & Hirschman, E. C. (1982, September). The experiential aspects of consumption: Consumer fantasies, feelings and fun. *Journal of Consumer Research, 9,* 132-140.

Holbrook, M. B., & Hirschman, E. C. (1992). *The semiotics of consumption.* Berlin: Mouton de Gruyter.

Holbrook, M. B., & Huber, J. (1983). Detecting the differences in jazz: A comparison of methods for assessing perceptual veridicality in applied aesthetics. *Empirical Studies of the Arts, 1*(1), 35-53.

Holbrook, M. B., & O'Shaughnessy, J. (1988). On the scientific status of consumer research and the need for an interpretive approach to studying consumer behavior. *Journal of Consumer Research, 15,* 398-402.

Holland, N. N. (1973). *Poems in persons: An introduction to the psychoanalysis of literature.* New York: Norton.

Huber, J. (1975, August). Predicting preferences on experimental bundles of attributes: A comparison of models. *Journal of Marketing Research, 12,* 290-297.

Hudson, L. A., & Ozanne, J. L. (1988, March). Alternative ways of seeking knowledge in consumer research. *Journal of Consumer Research, 14,* 508-521.

Hume, D. (1974). An enquiry concerning human understanding. In *The empiricists* (pp. 307-430). Garden City, NY: Anchor Books.

Hunt, S. D. (1983). *Marketing theory: The philosophy of marketing science.* Homewood, IL: Richard D. Irwin.

Hunt, S. D. (1984). Should marketing adopt relativism? In P. F. Anderson & M. J. Ryan (Eds.) *Scientific method in marketing* (pp. 30-34). Chicago: American Marketing Association.

Hunt, S. D. (1989). Naturalistic, humanistic and interpretive inquiry: Challenges and ultimate potential. In E. C. Hirschman (Ed.), *Interpretive consumer research* (pp. 185-198). Provo, UT: Association for Consumer Research.

Husserl, E. (1960). *Cartesian meditations: An introduction to phenomenology.* Atlantic Highlands, NJ: Humanities Press.

Hyde, L. (1983). *The gift: Imagination and the erotic life of property.* New York: Vintage Books.

Iser, W. (1978). *The act of reading.* Baltimore: Johns Hopkins University Press.

Juhl, P. D. (1980). *Interpretation: An essay in the philosophy of literary criticism.* Princeton, NJ: Princeton University Press.

Kant, I. (1929). *The critique of pure reason* (N. K. Smith, Trans.). London: MacMillan.

Kripke, S. A. (1982). *Wittgenstein on rules and private language.* Cambridge, MA: Harvard University Press.

Kuhn, T. S. (1970). *The structure of scientific revolutions* (2nd ed.). Chicago: The University of Chicago Press.

Kurzweil, E. (1980). *The age of structuralism: Lévi-Strauss to Foucault.* New York: Columbia University Press.

Langer, S. K. (1953). *Feeling and form.* New York: Scribner.

Langfitt, T. W., Hackney, S., Fishman, A. P., & Glowasky, A. V. (Eds.). (1983). *Partners in the research enterprise: University-corporate relations in science and technology.* Philadelphia: University of Pennsylvania Press.

Leiter, K. C. (1980). *A primer on ethnomethodology.* New York: Oxford University Press.

Lentricchia, F. (1980). *After the new criticism.* Chicago: University of Chicago Press.

Lévi-Strauss, C. (1960). Four Winnebago myths. In S. Diamond (Ed.), *Culture and history* (pp. 351-62). New York: Columbia University Press.

Lévi-Strauss, C. (1963). *Structural anthropology.* New York: Basic Books.

Lévi-Strauss, C. (1968a). *The origin of table manners.* New York: Harper and Row.

Lévi-Strauss, C. (1968b). *The raw and the cooked.* New York: Harper and Row.

Lévi-Strauss, C. (1978). *Myth and meaning.* New York: Schocken Books.

Lévi-Strauss, C. (1985). *The view from afar* (J. Neugroschel & P. Hoss, Trans.) New York: Basic Books.

Levine, D. N. (1985). *The flight from ambiguity: Essays in social and cultural theory.* Chicago: University of Chicago Press.

Levy, S. J. (1981, Summer). Interpreting consumer mythology: A structural approach to consumer behavior. *Journal of Marketing, 45,* 49-62.

Lincoln, Y. S., & Guba, E. G. (1985). *Naturalistic inquiry.* Beverly Hills, CA: Sage.

Locke, J. (1974). An essay concerning human understanding. In *The empiricists* (pp. 7-133). Garden City, NY: Anchor Books.

Lukacs, G. (1963). *The meaning of contemporary realism.* London: Merlin.

Lukacs, G. (1965). *Essays on Thomas Mann.* New York: Grosset & Dunlap.

Lukacs, G. (1971). *The theory of the novel.* London: Merlin.

Lukacs, G. (1974). *Soul and form.* London: Merlin.

MacQuarrie, J. (1972). *Existentialism.* New York: World.

Makkreel, R. A. (1975). *Dilthey: Philosopher of the human studies.* Princeton, NJ: Princeton University Press.

Mannheim, K. (1936). *Ideology and utopia.* London: Routledge & Kegan Paul.

Mannheim, K. (1952). *Essays on the sociology of knowledge,* London: Routledge & Kegan Paul.

Marx, K. (1970). *Capital: A critique of political economy* (Vol. 1). London: Lawrence and Wishart.

Marx, K. (1973). *Grundrisse.* Harmondsworth, UK: Penguin.

Marx, K., & Engels, F. (1968). *Selected works.* London: Lawrence and Wishart.

Marx, K., & Engels, F. (1978). *On literature and art.* Moscow: Progress.

McCarthy, E. J. (1971). *Basic marketing* (4th ed.). Homewood, IL: Richard D. Irwin.

McCracken, G. (1988). *The long interview.* Newbury Park, CA: Sage.

Melden, A. I. (1967). *Free action.* London: Routledge & Kegan Paul.

Mick, D. G. (1986, September). Consumer research and semiotics: Exploring the morphology of signs, symbols and significance. *Journal of Consumer Research, 13,* 196-213.

Mick, D. G. (1988). Contributions to the semiotics of marketing and consumer research. In T. Sebeok & J. Umiker-Sebeok (Eds.), *The Semiotic Web: A Yearbook of Semiotics* (pp. 535-584). Berlin: Mouton de Gruyter.

Miles, M. B., & Huberman, A. M. (1984). *Qualitative data analysis.* Newbury Park, CA: Sage.

Milgram, S. (1975). *Obedience to authority: An experimental view.* New York: Harper & Row.

Mills, C. W. (1956). *The power elite.* New York: Oxford University Press.

Morgan, G., & Smircich, L. (1980). The case for qualitative research. *Academy of Management Review, 5* (4), 491-500.

Morris, C. (1946). *Signs, language and behavior,* New York: George Braziller.

Morris, C. (1964). *Signification and significance: A study of the relations of signs and values.* Cambridge, MA: MIT Press.

Muncy, J. A., & Fisk, R. P. (1987, January). Cognitive relativism and the practice of marketing science. *Journal of Marketing, 51*, 20-33.

Myers, J. G., Massy, W. F., & Greyser, S. A. (1980). *Marketing research and knowledge development.* Englewood Cliffs, NJ: Prentice-Hall.

Neslin, S. A. (1981, February). Linking product features to perceptions: Self-stated versus statistically revealed importance weights. *Journal of Marketing Research, 18*, 80-86.

Northrop, F.S.C. (1947). *The logic of the sciences and the humanities.* Woodbridge, CT: Ox Bow Press.

Osgood, C. E., Suci, G. J., & Tannenbaum, P. H. (1957). *The measurement of meaning.* Urbana: University of Illinois Press.

O'Shaughnessy, J. (1987). *Why people buy.* New York: Oxford University Press.

Outhwaite, W. (1975). *Understanding social life: The method called verstehen.* New York: Holmes & Meier.

Ozanne, J. L. & Hudson, L. A. (1989). Exploring diversity in consumer research. In E. C. Hirschman (Ed.), *Interpretive consumer research* (pp. 1-9). Provo, UT: Association for Consumer Research.

Peckham, M. (1965). *Man's rage for chaos: Biology, behavior, and the arts.* New York: Schocken.

Peirce, C. S. (1955). *Philosophical writings of Peirce.* New York: Dover Publications.

Peter, J. P., & Olson, J. C. (1983, Fall). Is science marketing? *Journal of Marketing, 47*, 111-125.

Peter, J. P., & Olson, J. C. (1989). The relativist/constructionist perspective on scientific knowledge and consumer research. In E. C. Hirschman (Ed.), *Interpretive consumer research* (pp. 24-28). Provo, UT: Association for Consumer Research.

Plato (1968). *The republic* (B. Jowett, Trans.). New York: Airmont.

Polanyi, M. & Prosch, H. (1975). *Meaning.* Chicago: University of Chicago Press.

Popper, K. (1959). *The logic of scientific discovery.* New York: Harper Torchbooks.

Propp, V. (1968). *Morphology of the folktale* (2nd ed.). Austin: University of Texas Press.

Reagan, C. E. & Stewart, D. (1978). *The philosophy of Paul Ricoeur.* Boston: Beacon Press.

Ricoeur, P. (1965). *History and truth.* Evanston, IL: Northwestern University Press.

Ricoeur, P. (1971). The model of the text: Meaningful action considered as a text. *Social Research, 38*, 529-562.

Ricoeur, P. (1973). The task of hermeneutics. *Philosophy Today, 17*(2-4), 112-28.

Ricoeur, P. (1976). *Interpretation theory: Discourse and the surplus of meaning.* Fort Worth: Texas Christian University Press.

Ricoeur, P. (1981). *Hermeneutics and the human sciences: Essays on language, action and interpretation* (J. B. Thompson, Ed. and Trans.) Cambridge: Cambridge University Press.

Robertson, T. S. & Gatignon, H. (1986, March). A propositional inventory for new diffusion research. *Journal of Consumer Research, 11*, 849-867.

Rochberg-Halton, E. (1986). *Meaning and modernity: Social theory in the pragmatic attitude.* Chicago: University of Chicago Press.

Rogers, E. M. (1987). The critical school and consumer research. In M. Wallendorf & P. Anderson (Eds.), *Advances in consumer research* (Vol. 14, pp. 7-11). Provo, UT: Association for Consumer Research.

Rorty, R. (1979). *Philosophy and the mirror of nature.* Princeton, NJ: Princeton University Press.

Rorty, R. (1982). *Consequences of pragmatism.* Minneapolis: University of Minnesota Press.

Russell, B. (1945). *A history of western philosphy.* New York: Simon & Schuster.

Sapir, E. (1949). *Selected writings in language, culture and personality* (D. G. Mandelbaum, Ed.). Berkeley: University of California Press.

Sartre, J. P. (1950). *What is literature?* London: Methuen.

Sartre, J. P. (1956a). *Being and nothingness* (H. Barnes, Trans.) New York: Philosophical Library.

Sartre, J. P. (1956b). Existentialism is a humanism. In W. Kaufmann (Ed.), *Existentialism from Dostoevsky to Sartre.* New York: Meridian.

Sartre, J. P. (1963). *The problem of method.* London: Methuen.

Saussure, F. de (1959). *Course in general linguistics.* New York: McGraw-Hill.

Schleiermacher, F.D.E. (1978). The hermeneutics: Outline of the 1819 lectures (J. Wojik & R. Haas, Trans.). *New Literary History, 10*(1), 1-16.

Scholes, R. (1974). *Structuralism in literature.* New Haven, CT: Yale University Press.

Scholes, R. (1982). *Semiotics and interpretation.* New Haven, CT: Yale University Press.

Schutz, A. (1964). *Collected papers* (Vol. 2). The Hague: Martinus Nijhoff.

Schutz, A., & Luckmann, T. (1974). *The structure of the life world.* London: Heinemann.

Schweder, R. A. (1984). Anthropology's romantic rebellion against the Enlightenment, or there's more to thinking than reason and evidence. In R. A. Schweder & R. A. LeVine (Eds.), *Culture theory: Essays on mind, self, and emotion* (pp. 27-66). Cambridge: Cambridge University Press.

Scruton, R. (1981). *From Descartes to Wittgenstein.* New York: Harper & Row.

Scruton, R. (1982). *Kant.* Oxford: Oxford University Press.

Sebeok, T. A. (1981). *The play of musement.* Bloomington: Indiana University Press.

Seung, T. K. (1982). *Structuralism and hermeneutics.* New York: Columbia University Press.

Sherry, J. F. (1991). Postmodern alternatives: The interpretive turn in consumer research. In H. Kassarjian & T. Robertson (Eds.), *Handbook of consumer behavior* (pp. 548-591). Englewood Cliffs, NJ: Prentice-Hall.

Sperber, D. (1975). *Rethinking symbolism* (A. L. Morton, Trans.). Cambridge: Cambridge University Press.

Sperber, D. (1985). *On anthropological knowledge: Three essays.* Cambridge: Cambridge University Press.

Sperber, D. (1987). *On anthropological knowledge.* Cambridge: Cambridge University Press.

Sturrock, J. (Ed.). (1979). *Structuralism and since: From Lévi-Strauss to Derrida.* Oxford: Oxford University Press.

Taylor, C. (1985). *Philosophy and the human sciences.* Cambridge: Cambridge University Press.

Thompson, C. J., Locander, W. B., & Pollio, H. R. (1989, September). Putting consumer experience back into consumer research: The philosophy and method of existential phenomenology. *Journal of Consumer Research, 16,* 133-146.

Thompson, C. J., Locander, W. B., & Pollio, H. R. (1990, December). The lived meaning of free choice. *Journal of Consumer Research, 17*, 346-361.

Thompson, J. B. (1981). *Critical hermeneutics: A study in the thought of Paul Ricoeur and Jürgen Habermas*. Cambridge: Cambridge University Press.

Tybout, A. M., & Hauser, J. R. (1981, Summer). A marketing audit using a conceptual model of consumer behavior: Application and evaluation. *Journal of Marketing, 45*, 82-101.

Veblen, T. (1967). *The theory of the leisure class*. Harmondsworth, UK: Penguin.

Vico, G. (1976). *The new science* (T. G. Bergin & M. H. Fisch, Trans.) (3rd ed.). Ithaca, NY: Cornell University Press.

Williams, R. (1965). *The long revolution*. Harmondsworth, UK: Penguin.

Williams, R. (1973). Base and superstructure in Marxist cultural theory. *New Left Review, 82*, 3-16.

Williams, R. (1977). *Marxism and literature*. Oxford: Oxford University Press.

Williams, R. (1979). *Politics and letters*. London: New Left Books.

Wittgenstein, L. (1958). *Philosophical investigations* (G.E.M. Anscombe, Trans.). (3rd ed.). New York: Macmillan.

Wolff, J. (1975). *Hermeneutic philosophy and the sociology of art*. London: Routledge & Kegan Paul.

Wolff, J. (1981). *The social production of art*. New York: St. Martin's.

INDEX

ABOUT THE AUTHORS

Elizabeth C. Hirschman is Professor of Marketing, School of Business, Rutgers University. She has published articles in a wide variety of social science and business journals including the *Journal of Consumer Research, Journal of Marketing, Journal of Marketing Research, Journal of Business, Journal of Advertising Research, Journal of Advertising, Harvard Business Review, Semiotica, Journal of Retailing,* and *Psychology and Marketing.* Her primary research interests are philosophy of science, interpretive research methods and the semiotic analysis of cultural media. She is a past president and treasurer of the Association for Consumer Research and past vice-president of the American Marketing Association. She is a member of Kappa Tau Alpha, Phi Kappa Phi and Beta Gamma Sigma.

Morris B. Holbrook is the Dillard Professor of Marketing in the Graduate School of Business at Columbia University. He earned his bachelor's degree in English at Harvard in 1965. Both his MBA (1967) and Ph.D. (1975) are in Marketing from the Columbia

Business School. Holbrook's research applies a broad range of methods from the social sciences and humanities to issues related to communication, consumer esthetics, semiotics, hermeneutics, and other aspects of symbolic behavior. He has published widely in the areas of marketing and consumer research on topics related to the media, entertainment, advertising, and the arts.